LOVE FROM THE INSIDE OUT

LOVE FROM THE INSIDE OUT

lessons and inspiration for loving your life,
yourself, and each other

BY ROBERT MACK, *MAPP*

mango
PUBLISHING GROUP
CORAL GABLES

Love From the Inside Out: Lessons and Inspiration for Loving Yourself, Your Life, and Each Other

Library of Congress Cataloging-in-Publication number: 2021934507
ISBN: (print) 978-1-64250-352-4, (ebook) 978-1-64250-353-1
BISAC category code PSY016000, PSYCHOLOGY / Human Sexuality
(see also SOCIAL SCIENCE / Human Sexuality)

Printed in the United States of America

TABLE OF CONTENTS

PREFACE

LOVE IS NOT WHAT YOU THINK.

In fact, it's not what anybody thinks.

Love is what happens when you *don't* think—when you don't judge, when you don't expect, when you don't complain, and when you don't create stories in your head about what should or should not be happening in your life, especially your love life.

Love is an *experience* that unfolds easily, effortlessly, and enjoyably when you let go of thinking. It's an *experience* that manifests instantly when you let go of your thoughts, opinions, and beliefs about what should-be—what you should be, what your partner should be, what your relationships should be, what the world should be, what *everything* should be—and simply accept what is.

This book invites you to stop thinking and start living. It invites you to stop worrying about the past and future and start enjoying the present—your presence, other people's presence, and presence itself.

The truth is that we all work too hard at love. We work too hard at loving people, and we work too hard at being loved by people. We work too hard at all of our relationships, and the evidence is out: It's not working.

Love—real love—is easier than that, and it's more enjoyable than that, too.

This book invites you into an entirely different experience of love. It invites you into an experience of love that is easier and more enjoyable.

This book is intended to help you find true love and fulfillment, whether you are in a relationship or not. It's intended to help you taste real love right here and now, not one day in a future that never arrives.

Whether you're single, dating, in a relationship, or married, this book will help you transform your relationship with yourself and everybody else in the world into something happy, healthy, and harmonious.

The premise of this book is simple: When you change the way you relate with the world, the world changes the way it relates with you. When you find love inside yourself, you find love outside yourself, too. When you find love within, you find love wherever you go! You feel it for—and from—everybody else, even if they don't feel it for you.

Love from the Inside Out takes the form of individual entries organized into eleven topic clusters that range from "One with Life" to "Communication & Communion." Each entry is concise and complete in itself but, when read together, take on a transformative power.

After reading each entry, let there be a moment of silence so the truth of what's being said can sink into your heart, not just your head. The transformative power of these meditations can only be found and felt in stillness and silence, the same place from which they were written.

No thinking, no judging, no analyzing, no examining, no trying to figure anything out—just silence.

The teachings in this book are devices; they are pointers to the truth. They are signposts for the thoughtless, wordless awareness of peace, love, and joy that already exists inside you.

INTRODUCTION

EVERYBODY IS LOOKING FOR LOVE.

I've never met anybody who wasn't looking for love—in one way or another, in one place or another, or in one person or another.

Everybody wants to be loved.

I've never met anybody who didn't want to be loved. Whether they were looking for money, power, fame, a relationship, children, or something else, everybody wants to be—and really *feel*—loved.

No matter what we think we are looking for in life, we all just want to love and be loved. Isn't that true?

This book is about love, *real* love. And real love starts with self-love. When you love yourself, you love others without effort. When you love yourself, you love other people without trying.

Likewise, when other people love themselves, they love you without effort. When other people love themselves, they love you—and everybody else—without trying.

Real love is just self-love, *shared*. Love is sharing the love that you each found within yourself with each other. When you love yourself, you love other people automatically, and those people—if they are also full of self-love—love you back automatically.

Real love is just happiness, *shared*. Love is sharing the happiness that you each found within yourself with each other. When you are happy, you love other people automatically, and those people—if they are also full of happiness—love you back automatically.

Real love just requires one thing, then: getting out of your own way. To get out of your own way, you simply have to learn to stop thinking yourself out of love. You just have to learn to quiet your mind—to stop analyzing, stop examining, stop evaluating, stop complaining, stop judging, and stop trying to figure everything out in your life, especially in your love life.

When you learn to quiet your mind, you are self-loving instantly; you are happy instantly; you love others instantly; and others—if they are genuinely happy and self-loving, too—start loving you back instantly, too.

With one master key, all doors to life and love are unlocked. Quieting your mind even for one moment—what is sometimes called "meditation" or "practicing the Presence"—is the miracle of all miracles.

In other words, when you learn to quiet your mind, you immediately start loving yourself. When you start loving yourself, you become happy—even without a partner. When you become happy without a partner, you're happy, and that's the point of it all anyway, right?

But also, when you're happy, partners become infinitely more available to you, too. They show up out of nowhere, out of "now-here"—out of the present, out of presence itself.

Simply put, being happy makes everybody easier to love. When you are happy, it is easier for you to love other people, because *other people* are easier to get along with; and when you are happy, it is easier for other people to love you, too, because *you* are easier to get along with.

In fact, science has found that happy people are kinder, more charitable, more generous, and easier to get along with than unhappy people.

Moreover, research has also discovered that happy people are rated as more attractive, get married earlier, stay married longer, and are happier in all of their relationships, whether they are married or not, compared to their unhappy counterparts.

Happiness is attractive, literally and figuratively!

This book has one main premise, then: If you want to find a partner, you have to learn how to be happy without a partner. When you're happy without a partner, a partner is infinitely easier to attract... and keep!

The key to life and love, then, is just this: "How can I learn to stop thinking myself out of happiness, the happiness that is already inside me? How can I learn to be happy without a partner, so I can attract a partner?"

When you prioritize happiness above all else in this way, you're not only happy when you attract or find a partner—you're happy even in the process of attracting or finding a partner. You're happy even while you wait to find or attract a partner. You're happy even if you don't currently have—and never have—a partner!

In other words, you're happy no matter what. And isn't that the point of a partner—and everything else you think you want—anyway: to be happy?

Happiness is the key to finding love. And quieting your mind is the key to finding happiness.

So, in a nutshell, that's what this book is about. It's about learning how to love yourself and be happy. When you love yourself and are happy, you automatically love others without expecting anything in return. And when you love others without expecting anything in return, most people—the people who are self-loving and happy themselves—start loving you back. It really is that simple.

Happy reading, lovers!

Chapter 1

ONE WITH LIFE

You don't have a life—you **are** life.

You are one with life.

Feeling this—that you are one with life—**is** love.

Love is just felt oneness with life itself.

LOVE IS DIVINE

Love is divine.

It is the greatest miracle. It is the greatest blessing,
benediction, and bliss that exists.

Love is the highest religion.

All scripture—the Bible, the Torah, the Koran, and
the Gita—are just one thing: love.

Religions differ in their beliefs, but in the humble harmony of our hearts
and in the silent serenity of our soul, we are all the same: We are all love.

When you are love, you are truly religious, whether you belong to a religion or not.

Love makes all the scriptures come alive.

To know love is to know all the scriptures, and to *be*
love is to have fulfilled all the scriptures.

When you *are* love, you have *become* the scriptures. Love turns everybody
into a walking sermon. Love turns everybody into the living word. To
know love is to know the essence of everything that God knows.

To know love is to know the very aim and end of life, the primary
point and purpose of human existence. There is no higher
knowledge and no greater experience in the world than love.

"What is your religion," you ask?

"Love is my religion."

I'll leave it at that.

LOVE IS THE ANSWER

There are billions of problems in the world, but they
all boil down to just one: not enough love.

Think about it: Is there any problem in the world that more love couldn't solve?

There's only one problem in the world: People don't love each other enough... or at
all. We think we do, but we really don't. Most of us don't know what *real* love is.

Erich Fromm says, "Love is the only sane and satisfactory
answer to the problem of human existence."

According to the UN, 25,000 people die from starvation
every day. 10,000 of those people are children.

Believe it or not, there is enough food in the world right now to feed the
world's population several times over. Why, then, are people starving?

We have the money, resources, and scientific understanding to relieve the
world of so much unnecessary pain and suffering. So, why don't we?

Three words: Lack. Of. Love.

No matter what people say, a lack of money is not the real problem
in the world. There is enough money in the world, but there is
not enough love in the world. There are enough resources in the
world, but there is not enough *sharing* of those resources.

A lack of love has brought the world a lot more pain and
suffering than a lack of money has any day.

Do you really want to help the world?

Then, love the world!

ONE WITH LIFE

You don't have a life—you *are* life.

You don't only live a life—life lives *you!*

You live in God, yes, but God lives in *you*, too!

The drop isn't just in the ocean—the ocean is in the drop, too!

It sounds contradictory, but it's true: You and life—what I call "God"—are one.

Since you are one with Source, you are everything that Source is.

Source is silence, stillness, and spaciousness, so you
are silence, stillness, and spaciousness, too.

Source is infinite intelligence, so you are infinite intelligence, too.

Source is peace, love, and joy, so you are peace, love, and joy, too!

•

THE AIM AND END

Love is the entire meaning and purpose of life, the
whole aim and end of human existence.

Life is for living, and life is for loving.

If you miss love, you've missed life completely.

Life is the very peak and pinnacle of human experience.

Unless you've loved, your entire life has been wasted.

The purpose of life is love—felt oneness with life and all life forms.
When you have become love—when you realize that you *are* love—
you have fulfilled the fundamental purpose of your life.

You have attained; you have realized. You have attained
everything, and there is nothing left to attain.

ALWAYS STANDING ON THE GOAL

With love, you are always standing on the goal—you just
don't know it, and knowing it is everything!

In other words, love is always where you are—no matter
where you are—because you are there!

In fact, everything you could ever want or need is always right where you are,
no matter where you are, because you are one with the source of everything.

Anytime you go out into the world looking for love, or anything else for that matter,
you are missing the point. You are missing the mark, because you *are* the mark.

To "sin" means, literally, to "miss the mark." When you forget that you
are one with the infinite, eternal source within, you have "sinned."

Love—finding love and feeling loved—means knowing this:
"I am one with life and all life forms, and nothing can change
that. Not even so-called 'death' can change that."

Feeling anything less than love toward yourself or anybody else means
forgetting this simple truth: "Life and I are one. We cannot be separated...
ever. The true "I" of me is life. The real "I" of me is "God."

No matter what we do or where we go, we are always standing on
the goal, because we *are* the goal. We *are* the destination.

There is nowhere else to go.

If you would stop trying to run from this moment or another moment, you
would find that everything you are looking for is right here inside you.

Jesus says, "The kingdom of heaven is within."

Buddha says, "The way is not in the sky. The way is in the heart."

You can't escape life, no matter how fast or far you run, so you can't escape
love—*felt oneness with life and all life forms*—no matter where you hide.

That which you seek, you already have. In fact, that which you seek, you already *are*.

Knowing this—experiencing this for yourself—*is* peace, love, and happiness, too.

ACHIEVING NOTHING

This is going to sound a little crazy at first, but it's not...

When you attain love, you attain nothing.

You achieve nothing. You simply realize what has always been the case. You simply acknowledge what you have always been: one with life and everybody and everything in life.

At the deepest level, to know yourself as life is really not to know anything new at all. It's simply to remember what has always been the case.

True love is not achieved, attained, or acquired— it is simply acknowledged and accepted.

True love is not an achievement, attainment, or acquisition of a partner, a relationship, or anything else. It is simply remembering—and feeling—who and what you really are.

True love is simply waking up to your true nature.

•

LOVE MAKES LIFE MEANINGFUL

Love is the greatest gift life has given us.

In a way, love is even greater than life, because love makes life meaningful. Life only becomes meaningful when it becomes loving.

Life is the opportunity—love is its realization! Life is the potential—love is its fulfillment!

Love gives life meaning. Without love, there is no meaning to your life. There is no context for understanding your life.

You are a single note—love is the entire song! You are a single instrument— love is the whole symphony! You are a single line of poetry—love is the entire poem! You are a single page in a book—love is the whole book!

A single note, a single line, and a single page—they have no meaning, no beauty, and no bliss without the larger context.

Love is that larger context.

ONLY LOVE IS REAL

You are one with life (God).

Unhappiness is felt when you forget what you really are;
and happiness is felt when you remember what you really are.

Fear and loneliness are a function of forgetting your true Self,
and love is the result of remembering your true Self.

Fear is your false identity, and love is your true identity.

Indeed, we all experience non-love, non-peace, and non-joy at times, and we shall
do so until the day we die, because we all sometimes forget what we really are.

Life is all there is; God is all there is.

Only oneness is real—everything else is an illusion.

A *Course in Miracles* says, "Nothing real can be threatened.
Nothing unreal exists. Herein lies the peace of God."

Indeed, only love is real; only love exists.

True love can never be threatened because life—
and felt oneness with life—is all there is.

FALLING IN LOVE

There is only one problem in the world: a belief in separation.

All problems in the world can be reduced to one: perceived or illusory separation.

Separation is always an illusion; it is never real. Only oneness is real.

Love means knowing (feeling) this; fear means forgetting (not feeling) this.

Felt oneness with life (God) is love and felt separation from life (God) is fear.

You can never be separated from life (God)—even for a single moment, no matter what you or anybody else does (or doesn't do) to you—because you are life (God).

You can *think* you are separate or can be separated from life, but that's just a thought. It's not reality.

Buddhists call this realization "no self." You have no self—*no separate self*— that is or could ever be cut off from life. That's the ultimate realization.

When you believe that you are—or could ever be—separate from life or anything or anybody in life, you are living in fear. You are living in what people call "the ego."

That's what the ego is: a belief in separation. "The ego" just means "feeling separate and unloved."

Buddha is right. "In separateness lies the world's greatest misery; in compassion lies the world's true strength."

In love—in the recognition of your oneness with life and all life forms—lies your true power.

TRUE LOVE FEARS NOT AND WANTS NOT

True love fears not, and true love wants not.

True love fears nothing, and true love desires nothing, because true love is one with everything, one with the source of everything.

"The Father and I are one... The kingdom of heaven is within you... All that the Father has is mine."

You are one with the source of everything. You aren't missing a single thing—what is there to fear... or want?

I repeat: You have—in fact, you *are*—everything, the source of everything. For goodness sake, what's left to fear... or desire?

Buddha is right: "The whole secret of existence is to have no fear..." or desire (unhappy craving)!

When you have no fear or desire—because you know you are one with the source of everything—you have love already.

In fact, you *are* love already.

Lao Tzu says, "When there is no desire, all things are at peace."

When there is no fear and no desire, all things are in love.

In fact, all things *are* love.

YOU ARE THE SOURCE OF LOVE

Rilke says, "Believe in a love that is being stored up for you like an inheritance, and have faith that in this love there is a strength and a blessing so large that you can travel as far as you wish without having to step outside it."

The love that Rilke speaks of is in *you*, not the world.

In fact, the love that he speaks of *is* you, not anybody or anything else.

The key, then, is not to seek love in the world, but to find the source of love within yourself. You are the source of love, not the world or other people.

When you discover the love within yourself, you don't have to find love, because love finds you. When you stop chasing love, love chases you.

When you find the love that's inside you—that *is* you—you don't have to search for your soulmate, because suddenly *everybody* becomes your soulmate. Everywhere you look: another soulmate!

In other words, the truth is that love isn't impossible to find—love is impossible to avoid!

Notice how much love is inside you already. There is an inexhaustible source of love that exists inside each and every soul, which is really just one soul, already—just look for it! There's an infinitely deep wellspring of love inside you already—just dig for it!

You are one with the source of love, so you can always *be loving*, relationship or not. You can always be in love, partner or not.

In fact, you are always love, lover or not.

DON'T DRINK THE SALTWATER

Most people are looking for love in all the wrong places.

If you are looking for love outside yourself in the world—in other people, places, or things—you are looking for love in all the wrong places.

All *worldly* places are *wrong* places.

Looking for acceptance and approval from the world is fruitless. Seeking validation from other people, places, and things in the world—from a partner, a relationship, a marriage, or children—is hopeless.

The source is not out there in the world. The source is in you. In fact, the source *is* you.

In fact, I'd go so far as to say: If you're looking for peace, love, and happiness in the world—in other people, places, or things outside of yourself—you've given up on peace, love, and happiness altogether!

Looking for peace, love, and happiness out in the world is like trying to quench your thirst by drinking saltwater: The more you drink, the more you feel you need to drink.

The more you drink, the thirstier you become!

•

AN OCEAN OF LOVE

Are you having trouble finding love?

Can you imagine a fish looking for—and not finding—water?

A fish lives in water. For a fish, there is nothing but water. No water, no life. No water, no fish.

Fish live in water, and we live in an ocean, too. We live in an ocean of love, but we don't know it.

Love for us is like water for a fish: We can't escape it!

Each one of us lives in an ocean of love, and each one of us *is* an ocean of love, too.

No matter where you are, who you're with, or what you're doing, love is always right there with you, right there *in* you, right there *as* you.

GO WITHIN OR GO WITHOUT

Are you looking for peace, love, and happiness in all the wrong places?

Let me repeat: Every place outside of you is a wrong place. If you've been looking for peace, love, and happiness in the world—in other people, places, or things outside yourself—you've been knocking on all the wrong doors your entire life.

I can't say it enough: All *worldly* doors are *wrong* doors.

There's only one right door, and that door is *inside* you. Until you knock on that *inner* door—until you knock on your own heart and soul—you will never know the true treasures and real riches you've been carrying with you your whole life.

It sounds counter-intuitive, but it's true: The way *out* is *in*. The way *out* is through the *in-door*.

The way out of your unhappiness is within you. The way out of your loneliness and lovelessness is inside you. There is no way out—there is only a way in. Waaay in!

Always remember: *If you don't go within, you will go without.*

If you don't go within yourself to find peace, love, and happiness, you will never find peace, love, and happiness anywhere.

In the Gospel of Thomas, Jesus says, "If you bring forth what is within you, what you have will save you. If you do not bring it forth, what you do not [think you] have within you will kill you."

FINDING THE PERFECT MATE

I'm not teaching you how to *find* the perfect mate—I'm
teaching you how to *be* the perfect mate!

When you *are* the perfect mate, you always find the perfect mate, even
when they are imperfect, as all of us in human form ultimately are.

I'm *not* teaching you how to meet *somebody else* so that you can create an intense
love affair *for a little while*—I'm teaching you how to meet, melt, and merge with
yourself, your true Self, so that you can experience an intense love affair *all the time!*

When you meet, melt, and merge with your true Self—with that
thoughtless, wordless source of life and love inside you—every
interaction you have becomes an intense love affair.

This is what is sometimes called "meditation" or "practicing the Presence."

Meditation is just drowning in yourself—your true
Self, your divine Self, your God-Self.

It is drowning the false you in the ocean of love that you are.
It's drowning the false you—your ego—in love. It's drowning
your ego—your thoughts of separation—in God.

It just means drowning your thoughts in thoughtless, wordless, faceless,
formless awareness. It's drowning your thoughts in thoughtlessness.

It means feeling your oneness with life, the source of peace,
love, and happiness within. It means knowing that the soulmate
you've always been looking for and waiting for is *you.*

You are your own soulmate—only you don't know it!
You are your own *soul, mate*—just know it!

You and all others—with whom you are also one with in life (God)—are part
of the same soul, only you don't know it, and knowing it is everything.

In other words, don't worry about meeting "the one" and making
it work. Simply realize that you—and everybody else—are "The
One," and it's already working, only you don't know it!

Just know it.

NOTHING SUCCEEDS LIKE FAILURE

Nothing fails like success.

No matter how successful your life becomes, it is not real success unless you are fulfilled by it. Only *inner* success is *real* success. Only inner success fulfills you.

In other words, no matter how full your life becomes, the world will never be capable of "full-filling" you, because you can't stuff your insides with outer things.

No matter what you achieve, attain, or acquire, nothing in the world will—or can—fill a hole in your soul.

Jesus says, "What good is it to gain the world and lose your soul?"

Whatever you are looking for, unless you find it inside you already, you will never find it in the world.

Only that which you know is within you can ever be found in the world, because the world is simply an outer projection of what you have found inside you. The world is simply a mirror. It mirrors back to you what you see in yourself—happiness or unhappiness, peace or conflict, love or hate, success or failure, prosperity or poverty.

If you live with a feeling of inner emptiness—if you live from the ego—nothing will ever make you happy.

Your pockets may be full of money, but your eyes will be full of tears. Your life may be full of lovers, but your heart will be full of heartache.

Even with a lover intact, even with a lover in tow, your life will be lonely and loveless all the same.

The outer journey—the worldly, ego-driven *search for love*, approval, and acceptance—is not the real journey. The inner journey—the otherworldly, spiritual *journey of love*, approval, and acceptance—is the real journey.

When you take the inner journey, you come to realize that nothing succeeds like failure.

Nothing is more helpful for finding real peace, love, and happiness than discovering where it cannot be found. Nothing is more helpful to you than discovering that the world—other people, places, and things—can't fulfill you.

Nothing is more beneficial in the long-run than finding out that other people—even the best of lovers, even the best of relationships, and even the best of children—can't make you feel peaceful, loved, and happy all the time.

In other words, the failure of other people, places, and things (the world) to fulfill you—what is called "divine discontent"—can be a great help, because it can force you to finally look for peace, love, and happiness in the only place it can ever be found:

Inside you.

HUMAN LOVE AND DIVINE LOVE

Erich Fromm once said, " 'Love' is a relatively rare phenomenon,
and its place is taken by a number of forms of pseudo-love."

By "love," he means "divine love." By "pseudo-love," he means "human love."

If your love is based on anything temporary or limited, like other people
or circumstances, your love will be equally temporary and limited.

When the cause dissolves, so will the effect. When the root dies, so will the fruit.

If you want infinite, eternal, uncaused, and unconditional
love, it must be founded only on that which is infinite, eternal,
uncaused, and unconditional: life itself (God).

Divine love—felt oneness with life (God)—is infinite and eternal;
nothing can destroy it. The form that that divine love takes might
change over the course of time—the relationship might change or
evolve—but divine love, oneness with life (God), never dies.

The truth is this: Human love always fails—only divine love succeeds. Human
love always fails to fulfill you—only divine love always fulfills you!

This is good news because the failure of human love is the success of
divine love. The end of human love is the beginning of divine love.

The failure of human love to fulfill you is what leads you back to seek
and find divine love, the only kind of love that will always fulfill you.

Human love doesn't conquer all, after all, at all.

Only divine love conquers all, because it is the All, after all.

CELEBRATING SOULMATES

The pinnacle of human experience is to experience
your own soul and its oneness with all souls.

And yet, this experience is also the most ordinary, common experience
of all, because we are always experiencing nothing but our own soul
and its oneness with all souls. We are all always experiencing nothing
but the One Soul, because that's what we, in essence, truly are.

Only we don't consciously know it; we aren't consciously aware of it.

Knowing that oneness—feeling that oneness—is divine love.

It's both the ground and goal of all creation; it's both the
foundation and fulfillment of all existence.

"Namaste" means: "I honor the sacred place within you where—when (I know)
I am in mine, and you (know you) are in yours—there is only One of us."

A soulmate is the recognition of your soul—the same soul—in another. It is
the recognition of your true, divine Self—life or God—in another. Because
everybody is a part of that same soul, everybody is your soulmate.

Everybody is your soul; everybody is one in with the same soul.

When you celebrate soulmates, then, you're celebrating an inner marriage
in spiritual form. With outer marriage, separation is possible; but with inner
marriage, no separation is ever possible—oneness is its very nature.

In other words, when you discover the truth—that we are
all one—you discover your soulmate: all of us.

Rumi is right, "Lovers don't finally meet somewhere.
They are in each other all along."

We are *all* lovers, because we are all in each other all along.

IN LOVE WITH LIFE

When you truly, deeply love someone in the way that I mean it—at their spiritual core, at the formless level—you are, in reality, loving life itself.

You are loving God.

True love means feeling one with who and what a person is deep inside, in their spirit. It means feeling the presence of the One Life within that other person... and all other people.

True love means "seeing God" in the other. It means feeling life—the same life force, life energy, or presence of life—within the other.

In other words, "seeing God" just means feeling the divine aliveness within the other by feeling the divine aliveness within *yourself*.

To love another is to recognize your original "face"—the presence of life, the presence of God—in him or her. It's to recognize yourself—your true Self, your divine Self—in the other.

All true love is just the felt experience of the presence of life or God within yourself, which is the same life or God within everybody else, too.

All love is really the love of—and love for—life itself.

It is all just life loving itself; it's all just God loving God.

HUMANITY AND DIVINITY

It's by loving people that we express our divinity; and it's by realizing
our divinity that we are finally able to truly love people.

In other words, it's through our humanity that we discover our divinity,
and it is by discovering our divinity that we properly love humanity.

To discover the one formless life that underlies all life forms, you have to love
and accept the life forms themselves. You cannot discover the one formless
life that underlies all life forms by rejecting any of the individual life forms.

Put simply: To discover God within, you have to love and accept people; and
to accept and love people properly, you have to discover God within.

In other words, true love means both: loving people in their physical,
human form and loving people in their non-physical, spiritual form.

It means loving God in the manifest form and loving
God in the unmanifest form, too.

Jesus says it this way: "Love God with all your heart and with all your
soul and with all your mind. This is the first and greatest commandment.
And the second is like it: Love your neighbor as yourself."

Chapter 2

YOUR NATURAL STATE

Love is your true nature.

When you are relaxed, love is what you feel inside without trying at all—without thinking, saying, or doing anything at all.

Love is Being, just being.

LOVE IS NOT A RELATIONSHIP

Are you looking for love in a relationship?

Do you think you can only be in love—love others, be loved
by others, and feel loved—if you are in a relationship?

Love is not a relationship you have with one person—love
is a way you have of relating with the whole world!

Love is not a state of relationship—love is a state of *being*!

It is the way you conduct yourself with everybody in the whole
world, not just one or two people here and there.

Love is not a relationship—love is a *way of relating*!

•

LOVE IS NOT AN EMOTION

Do you fall in and out of love?

Do you feel love(d) at certain times but not at other times? Do you feel
love(d) on some occasions but not on other occasions? Do you feel
loving toward some people but not toward other people? Do you think
love is an emotion that comes and goes like a cloud in the sky?

Love is not an emotion. It's not something that comes and goes.
It's not something that visits for a while and then leaves.

No, real love comes and stays forever. It doesn't leave. It
settles down, moves in, and makes itself at home!

In truth, of course, real love has never left. It could never leave,
because real love has always had its home inside of you.

A gap between two wars is not real peace—it's just preparation for another
war. A gap between two miseries is not real happiness—it's just preparation
for more misery. And a gap between two periods of lovelessness or loneliness
is not real love—it's just preparation for more lovelessness and loneliness!

Love is not a state of mood—love is a state of being!
More accurately, love is Being itself.

Love is not what you feel sometimes—love is what you *are* all the time!

LOVE IS A QUALITY

True love is a *quality*.

It's a quality like friendliness, kindness, or compassion. It's the same quality that surrounds a Jesus, a Buddha, or a Lao Tzu.

True love—as a quality—only depends on *you*, not anybody else. With true love, you're always resting in and *as* love, so you're always coming from a place of love.

You're always loving, whether the situation seems to call for it or not.

(And it always calls for it, by the way.)

You're always loving, whether the person is lovable or not.

(And the person is always lovable, by the way.)

In other words, your love life—your ability to love and feel loved—*never* depends on anybody but you, because being kind, caring, and compassionate toward yourself and others is something that is always within your control.

Your love life has nothing to do with anybody else being lovable and everything to do with *you* being "love-able"—capable of loving yourself and others.

Anybody can love the lovable—can you love the unlovable? That's the question.

When you can answer "yes" to that question—when you can love even the unlovable—you have attained. That's true love.

In other words, loving the unlovable is the litmus test for true love.

Of course, "loving the unlovable" does *not* mean staying in an abusive or unhappy relationship. It does *not* mean being a pushover or a doormat. It does *not* mean sacrificing your own happiness for somebody else's happiness.

No, it doesn't mean any of this at all.

"Loving the unlovable" means attaining a level of awareness—resting in (as) thoughtless *awareness*—where it's actually easier and more enjoyable to love than not to love, to love yourself and others than not to love yourself and others.

It means attaining a state of being, your natural state of being where love is effortless.

It's automatic.

LOVE IS FOR EVERYBODY

True love is inclusive, not exclusive.

It's not discriminatory. It includes everybody and everything in it.

True love is not addressed or directed only to certain people—
it is unaddressed and undirected to *all* people.

It is for everybody!

True love is not a relationship with one person—it's a
way of relating with everybody in the world.

•

LOVE IS NOT ACQUIRED

Love isn't an achievement—it's an *acknowledgment*.

Love isn't reached—it's *recognized*.

Love isn't something you *do*—it's something you *are*.

Love isn't *acquired*—it's *allowed*.

When you are completely relaxed—at ease with yourself
and the world—love happens (is felt) all by itself.

LET IT FLY, LET IT FLOW!

Love is simple.

Love happens when you get out of your own way. Love happens
when you get out of life's way, when you get out of God's way.

Rumi says, "Your task is not to seek for love, but merely to seek and
find all the barriers within that you have built against it."

In other words, love is the disappearance of the illusory ego—your false sense
of a separate self, your false sense of separation from life and all life forms.

Love happens—and lovers appear—when you learn to drop your lonely, loveless
thoughts of separation and feel your underlying oneness with life and all life forms.

The key, then, isn't to force love to happen or lovers to appear—the key is simply
to relax and allow everything inside you that is non-loving to disappear.

Just get out of the way! Then, love will flow freely *from*
you, and lovers will flow freely *to* you!

Don't force love—let it flow.

Don't force love—*free* love, the love that is within you.

Don't seek love in the world—seek love within *yourself*.

Seek it within yourself by learning how to drop your lonely, loveless
thoughts of lack, separation, sadness, and suffering.

LET IT FLY, LET IT FLOW! (2)

When I was a child, I had a love affair with basketball.

I played basketball day-in and day-out, all day and all night. My dad and I built a basketball hoop in my driveway, and I would practice at that hoop as much as humanly possible.

Sometimes, my dad would come out and shoot baskets with me. When he did, he'd always say the same thing. He'd say, "Let it fly, son! Let it flow, boy!"

I had a hard time learning that lesson. I was too focused on making every shot. I was too focused on the end result.

By "Let it fly" and "Let it flow," he meant, "Relax and let it be natural." He meant, "Don't think—just shoot!" He meant, "Let go and let God."

Detach from the end result. Don't worry about making every shot—just enjoy the game!

"Let it fly, let it flow!" That's what I'm saying to you here, too.

Don't worry about "meeting somebody" and "making it work"—just enjoy yourself!

Just enjoy the company of whomever and whatever is in your life right now, even—and especially—if it's only yourself.

Let it flow, let it fly! Let the love flow, let the love fly!

The rest will take care of itself.

LOVE IS NOT FORCED

Love is divine.

It doesn't come *from* this world—it comes from *beyond* this world. It comes from the beyond, from life itself (God).

In other words, love doesn't come from you, the "you" that you know as the ego. It comes *through* you, but it comes *from* God within—the source of love within you.

Life comes *through* the flower, not from the flower; and love comes *through* you, not from you, the ego.

This must be understood. If it isn't understood, you will try to force love to happen through your thoughts, words, and actions.

Real love isn't forced or created by thinking, saying, and doing the right things—it's *freed* from within you by *being* the right thing.

More accurately, it's freed from within you by *Being* (God), by just being.

In other words, love happens when you are loose and natural inside. It happens when you are relaxed inside, when you are at ease with yourself and the world. It happens when you are just a transparency for life (God) to express itself through you, *as you.*

Just totally relax. Then, the divine can express itself through you, *as you.*

That's love.

•

TRUE LOVE IS FORMLESS

True love is formless.

It can take any form: romantic, platonic, professional, whatever. But at its heart—at the formless level—true love is always friendly, kind, and compassionate.

Friendliness, kindness, and compassion can be exercised in person or at a distance, inside a romantic relationship or outside of a romantic relationship.

I'll repeat it again: True love is a quality—a quality like friendliness, kindness, or compassion.

Friendship is the highest form of love; kindness and compassion are the highest kind of love!

RELAX

When you attain love, you attain nothing, because
whatever you attain was inside you all along.

Love isn't addition—it's subtraction.

Love isn't gaining anything—it's losing something.

You lose your ego—your false sense of separation. You lose your
worries, your anxieties, your regrets, and your stressful thoughts.

You lose everything that was in the way of love, and *that* is your achievement.

Love is breaking down the barriers inside you that
you have built against love, that's all.

Love is your nature, your true nature.

It is not something you strive for—it's something you relax *into*.

•

YOUR TRUE NATURE

Meditation makes you a mirror.

It allows you to see your face—your original face, your true nature, your loving
nature. It allows you to see your Buddha nature, your Christ consciousness.

It allows you to experience your oneness with life (God). It allows you
to realize yourself—and everybody else—*as* life itself (God).

In other words, it allows you to see your original face and everybody else's
original face—love—reflected back to you, despite whatever seemingly
unloving and unlovable things they might have done or be doing.

LOVE HAPPENS BY ITSELF

Let me repeat this: Never try to force love.

Never try to force yourself to be more loving; never try to force others to love you; and never try to force a relationship to work out.

Forced love is not real love, and it doesn't lead to real love, either. If you force anything, you will only be repressing its opposite, and that never works.

If you repress anything in an attempt to be more loving, to be more lovable, or to make a relationship work—if you repress hate, anger, jealousy, sadness, sex, or whatever it is that you think is getting in the way of your love life—those repressed qualities will only grow stronger.

Eventually, they will grow into a sort of cancer inside you.

Repressing things in the name of love simply hides the problem. If you hide a problem, you can't look into it, understand it, and transform it. You can only force it underground, where it will grow and fester, until one day it explodes.

In truth, even indulgence is better than repression. Even indulging is better than repressing, because indulgence, at least, lets you see the problem. When you see the problem, you can heal the problem.

Always remember: You can only understand and heal what you look into. You can't understand and heal what you hide. You have to expose a wound and seek the proper medical care to help it heal.

So, don't force yourself to be more loving or lovable; don't force others to be more loving or lovable; and don't try to force a relationship to work.

Instead, just learn how to relax inside and, then, as a result of that relaxation, you, your partner, and the whole world will become more loving, more lovable, and easier to get along with. Just try it and see.

In other words, we are all working too hard on relationships. We are all working too hard at being more loving and more lovable. We are all working too hard at finding a new lover or improving our current one. We are all working too hard on making everything work out in our lives.

If you can learn just one thing—if you can learn to take the path of least resistance by relaxing a little bit—everything will begin to take care of itself, and all your relationship problems will begin to solve themselves.

Learn to be in a state of let-go inside. When you are in a state of let-go or inner surrender, suddenly you will smell this beautiful fragrance coming from your core. That fragrance is love, and that fragrance will attract loving people from all walks of life to you.

So remember: Real love comes from the beyond. It's not something that you can force. The most you can hope for is that your relaxation—what I call your "meditation"—is right.

Then, love will spring up *out* of you. You will have so much love inside that you will have to share it with the world just to get rid of it!

Love is simply the consequence of a quiet mind; it is
the shadow of a silent and serene mind.

When you learn to relax, love grows effortlessly, and lovers find you easily—
and without all the unnecessary pain and suffering you're used to.

When you relax—for no reason at all, addressed to nobody in particular—love erupts from within you. Without cause, there is an inner explosion of light that you have never known before, and that light is reflected back to you from the world.

God has entered you. God has penetrated you, and you will never be the same again.

More accurately, you realize that God has never left you, because God has always lived inside of you—*as you*—and you are never the same again.

Love cannot be forced or coerced—it must be discovered
and rediscovered through relaxation.

Love is a by-product. It is the natural consequence of a quiet mind.

Don't force anything—just relax into everything.

When you are relaxed—when you get out of your own way, when you get out of life's way, when you get out of God's way—love happens all by itself.

WHO YOU REALLY ARE

Meditation makes you a silent pool, a pool without any waves or ripples.

Through meditation, you become still and silent inside. When you become still and silent inside, you are able to "see"—*experience* or *feel*—your divine nature.

"Seeing"—experiencing and feeling—your divine nature *is* peace, love, and joy.

Waves only exist on the surface. Unhappiness, confusion, and conflict only exist on the surface. When you dive more deeply into the ocean of yourself—the Self, God within—you find only peace, love, and joy.

When you learn to quiet all the mental chatter inside,
you experience divine peace, love, and joy.

And when you experience divine peace, love, and
joy inside, other people are drawn to it.

Dive deeply into the silent pool of your own being—*Being* itself,
Presence itself—and you'll discover something divine inside:

You aren't the wave—you are the water!

You aren't human—you are spirit!

You don't have a life—you *are* life!

You aren't separate from life—you are one with life!

You aren't separate from God—you are one with God!

The wave experiences ups and downs, coming and going, birth
and death. But the water experiences neither up nor down,
neither coming nor going, neither birth nor death.

No coming, no going, no birth, no death—that's reality.

When you experience this for yourself—that you are the water, not
the wave; that you are spirit, not human—your fear disappears.

And it's replaced with love.

Experiencing yourself as the water—and not just the wave—is the
purpose of meditation. Experiencing yourself as a spiritual being—
and not just a human being—is the practice of prayer.

Jesus calls it "resting in God."

It's relaxing into yourself—your true Self, your silent Self.

It's resting in peace, love, and joy.

It's experiencing oneness with everybody and everything.

It's experiencing true love—love for yourself, love for others, and
love for everything—without any conditions attached.

It's *being* love.

It means looking deeply into your divine nature to discover the peace, love, and
joy that is already inside you. It's discovering the peace, love, and joy that *is* you.

Unless you are in touch with the peace, love, and joy inside you—that *is* you—
your insight is not yet deep enough. The surface of your mind is still a little
choppy, so your perception into the depths of your soul is still a little shallow.

A lack of penetrating insight caused by too much thinking—and not
enough awareness—will always lead to non-peace, non-love, and
non-joy. When your insight is superficial, you can't experience the
reality of peace, love, and joy that exists beneath the surface.

When the sea is angry and the water is disturbed, the clouds are not reflected in
the water. You can't see the mirror image of the clouds in an ocean full of waves.

Likewise, when you're disturbed, you can't see your divine nature
reflected inside. You can't see the truth about yourself, other people,
or the world in a mind full of thoughts and judgments.

When you are disturbed, your mind is full of too many thoughts,
too much programming. It is full of too many judgments, opinions,
and beliefs about yourself, others, the world, and life itself.

All negative states—all non-love, non-peace, and non-joy—are
caused by too much thinking and not enough awareness. Too much
thinking—and not enough thoughtless awareness—always blocks
deep insight, true understanding, and divine wisdom.

It always blocks divine peace, love, and joy.

THINKING SEPARATES

Oneness is the reality.

Thinking is always divisive; it always separates.

To think is to separate. To *not* think is to retain the inherent oneness of all things.

This is the practice of love: not thinking.

Thoughtless awareness.

•

BECOMING CHILD-LIKE

Love requires you to become child-like.

To become "child-like" means to become innocent again. It's to become egoless.

It's to dismiss all your fearful, unhappy, unloving thoughts of lack and separation so that you become—or, rather, *so that you realize that you have always been*—trusting, loving, whole, complete, and one with All-That-Is.

When you are absolutely egoless and empty inside—"poor in spirit," so to speak—you realize you are filled with peace, love, and happiness. You become a living shrine, a living temple for divine peace, love, and happiness to enter.

Or, more accurately, *you realize that you have always been* a living shrine, a living temple where divine peace, love, and happiness live.

In other words, to become innocent or child-like means to die or disappear as your false, human self and be reborn or reappear as your true, spiritual Self.

It's simply remembering—*feeling*—your infinite and eternal oneness with life itself (God).

NEW DAY, NEW YOU

When you dive deeply enough inside yourself, you discover the source
of peace, love, and happiness within... and you drown in it.

The old you dies completely, and a new you is born. The anxious, unhappy,
unloving you dies, and the peaceful, happy, loving you is born.

The false you is crucified, and the real you—the *original* you—is resurrected. More
accurately, the false you is seen through, and the real you becomes evident.

Becoming love, then, is the death of the fearful, unloving mind, and the rebirth
of the trusting, loving heart. More accurately, it is seeing through the illusion
of the fearful, unloving mind to the reality of the trusting, loving heart.

That is the real meaning of rebirth and resurrection: dying to the
physical plane and being reborn on the spiritual one. It's being
crucified as a human being and resurrected as a spiritual being.

It's dying to the ego (the illusory, separate self) and being reborn as the non-ego (the
real Self, the "non-self," the Self that is never separate from anybody or anything).

The first birth is a physical birth, but the second is a spiritual one.

•

SELF-REALIZATION

The purpose of your life is to discover yourself.

It's to discover your real Self, the one Self: the thoughtless, wordless,
faceless, formless, infinite, eternal One Life that underlies all life forms.

When you discover yourself—your true Self, your spiritual Self,
the one Self, God within—you've found it all. You've found the
source of everything, including peace, love, and happiness.

You've realized yourself, the Self, God. You're Self-realized, God-realized.

Self-realization means knowing yourself, realizing yourself, or experiencing
yourself—even though it's not an "experience," per se—as life itself (God).

God-realization or Self-realization—felt oneness with life and all life forms—is the
whole aim and end of life, the whole meaning and purpose of human existence.

You can also simply call it "love."

I call it love, true love.

Chapter 3

YOUR HAPPINESS, SHARED

When you're happy, you love other people.

You don't have to try.

You just do.

LOVE IS HAPPINESS, SHARED

Love is your happiness, *shared*.

Misery shared is not misery divided—it's misery *multiplied*.

Happiness shared is not happiness divided—it's happiness *multiplied*.

To multiply your happiness, share the happiness you have.

That's the practice of love.

•

LOVE IS AN UNDERSTANDING

People think love is something you do:

"Love one another."

"Be more loving."

"Practice loving kindness."

"Be kinder to each other."

Love is not something you *do*—love is something you *are*.

Love is not a *discipline*—love is an *understanding*.

When you are happy, love happens automatically.

When you are happy, love already is.

LOVE IS BLISS OVERFLOWING

When you are so full of bliss that you can't contain it anymore, you
flood the whole world with it just to relieve yourself—that's love!

When you are so full of bliss that you can't hold on to it any longer, you
shower the whole earth with it just to unburden yourself—that's love!

A rain cloud can't contain its rain; a flower can't contain its fragrance; the
sun can't contain its sunlight; and blissful people can't contain their bliss.

Blissful people can't keep their love to themselves, no matter what they do.
Blissful people can't keep their bliss to themselves, no matter how hard they try.

When you are drenched in, dripping with, and coated with
blissfulness, you get it all over everything and everybody—no
matter where you go, what you do, or who you meet.

•

QUEEN OF JOY, EMPRESS IN LOVE

Love means knowing one thing: You can only share what you have.

If you are miserable, you only have misery to share—that's "hate."

If you are joyful, you only have joy to share—that's "love."

Love is just your joy, *shared*.

Only light can come from light; only hate can come from
misery; and only love can come from joy.

If you are the queen of sorrow, you will be a beggar in love.
Be a queen of joy, so you can be an empress in love!

In other words, unless you are joyful, forget all about love.

You are not ready yet.

RICH IN JOY, WEALTHY IN LOVE

True love is always happy, and true love is always free.

If it's not happy, it's not love—it's a burden.

If it's not free, it's not love—it's a prison sentence.

Give love happily and freely or not at all.

When it comes to love, never be a beggar—be a king!

A real king gives freely and joyfully. He has so much that he doesn't need to keep track of what he's given or to whom he's given it.

If you don't have joy, you are a beggar. And if the other doesn't have joy, he or she is a beggar, too. That makes two beggars, and two beggars in a relationship cannot make each other better off. They can only make each other worse off.

Before bliss, you have nothing but misery to give—that makes you a beggar.

Don't be a beggar in bliss and a beggar in love.

Become rich in bliss so that you can become wealthy in love! Become a king in bliss so that you can become an emperor in love!

•

TRUE LOVE IS ALWAYS FREE

True love is always free.

It never comes with a price tag. There's never any ambition or business in it. There's never any bargaining or negotiation in it.

If there are any strings attached to your love—if there is any motivation in your loving others, save joy—it is not true love.

True love is a luxury. It comes out of your abundance of joy. It is an overflow, an overflow of bliss.

Love is freedom, total freedom.

True love—the kind that grows organically out of bliss— gives of itself freely. It expects nothing in return.

Hafiz expresses this beautifully. He says, "Even after all this time, the Sun never says to the Earth, 'You owe me.' Look what happens with a love like that: It lights up the whole sky."

THE GIFT OF LIFE

Love starts with a simple understanding.

The greatest thing that could ever happen to anybody
has happened to you already: life itself.

You didn't earn it, and yet it happened to you. You didn't do
anything to deserve it, and still it happened to you.

When you understand that life is a gift that you never
earned, a feeling of gratitude grows in your heart.

That gratitude is love.

What have you ever earned of real value? If you were never born, could you
really say something wrong, unfair, or unjust had been done to you?

Life: You didn't earn it in the first place!

Everything we have in life is a gift we didn't earn, because life
itself is a gift we never earned. Everything is a gift given out
of God's grace. It is all a gift given out of divine love.

Your life, no matter what it contains, is beautiful. Your life is a blessing
and a benediction, no matter what it consists of. It is a miracle.

If not for grace, you would never have been born. You would have never been alive.

Because life loves you so much, it gave itself to you. It was only out
of deep, heartfelt love and generosity that it was given to you.

It could've been given to somebody else, but it was given to you. It
came with your name and face stamped on it. It is all for you.

Your life must be special. It must be valuable. It must be divine.

In fact, *you* must be special; *you* must be valuable; and *you* must be divine!

No matter what or who you are, you should be deeply grateful for your
life, because it is God-given. You are one of the chosen few.

Life loves you so much that it gave you—and continues to give
you—its most precious and prized possession of all: itself.

You are loved and adored by existence, by the whole, by life, by God—
what does it matter if you're not loved or accepted by anybody else?

Please always remember: If you are alive—and you will *always* be alive somewhere
because you *are* life itself—you are loved and accepted by existence, by life, by God.

No matter what you or anybody else thinks, there is no
greater love than that in the whole wide world!

STAY HOME

All lessons in love are really lessons in being happy.

Love is happy. If love isn't happy, it isn't love.

Never go to the grocery store when you're hungry, and never go looking for love when you're unhappy. Never go to the grocery store when your stomach is empty, and never go looking for love when your heart is empty.

If you do, you're going to acquire nothing but junk food. And you're only going to become unhealthier and, ultimately, unhappier; you're only going to become more miserable as a result.

Love that grows out of unhappiness will never fulfill you—it is empty calories. It will never satisfy you. Only organic love—love that grows naturally out of happiness—will satisfy you.

Only joy-based love is substantive. Only joy-based love is filling... and fulfilling!

Unless you are authentically happy, stay home and fill yourself up, first.

Before you go out into the world to find love, stay home and get your own house (happiness) in order.

As Rilke says, "For one human being to love another human being: That is perhaps the most difficult task that has been given to us, the ultimate, the final problem and proof, the work for which all other work is merely preparation."

DANCING WITH THE DIVINE

Love and happiness are inside jobs.

Please don't waste your whole life searching the world for
that perfect person, hoping that you'll find true love and
happiness hiding out there in the world somewhere.

You'll only find that the source of true love and fulfillment, in all her guts
and glory, has been carefully tucked away inside your own heart and soul.
She's been sweetly, safely, and soundly sleeping inside you all along, patiently
waiting for you to disturb her little slumber, so she can come out and play!

Don't look for love and happiness in the world—
look for love and happiness in *yourself!*

In fact, don't even look—just listen.

Quiet your mind and listen. In time, you will begin to hear this
divine music playing inside your own heart and soul.

Listen closely—that's Source strumming the strings of your heart.
Pay attention—God is playing divine music in your heart.

When you get this—when you really understand this—you will know what
Friedrich Nietzsche meant when he said, "Those who were seen dancing
were thought to be insane by those who could not hear the music."

Just listen.

In fact, don't even listen—just be silent.

Then, everything else will happen on its own... in divine timing...
by divine dispensation... according to divine destiny.

Franz Kafka says it this way, "You do not need to leave your room.
Remain sitting at your table and listen. Do not even listen, simply wait,
be quiet, still and solitary. The world will freely offer itself to you to
be unmasked, it has no choice, it will roll in ecstasy at your feet."

DRUNK WITH THE DIVINE

Be blissful.

Then, life will shower you with infinite blessings.

Love is simply the outer expression of somebody who lives
with deep inner gratitude, wonder, and awe.

Once you have attained—once you have experienced this deep gratitude for
the gift of life—you will automatically start sharing that bliss with the world.

You can't do otherwise.

A star can't keep its light to itself; a flower can't keep its fragrance
to itself; and you can't keep your bliss to yourself.

When you are drunk with the divine—with divine
bliss—your drunkenness is contagious.

That contagious bliss *is* love.

Get drunk with the divine, get drunk with God.

Then, you—and everybody you come into contact with—
will be filled with divine love in no time!

•

TRUE LOVE IS ALWAYS LOVING

When you are joyful, you don't have to be told to love people.

You don't have to be reminded to be more loving.
When you are joyful, love is automatic.

Do you have to be told to keep breathing?

Does the sun have to be told to keep shining?

Do the birds have to be reminded to keep singing?

No! And the same is true of you when you are joyful. When you
are joyful, love is not a choice—it's the natural consequence,
the automatic by-product of your state of being.

To let the light in, just don't block the sun. To let the love
in, just don't block the source (within you).

Love just means letting the light of divinity flow into,
through, and out of you... into the world.

LOVE-LOVE RELATIONSHIPS

When you are full of bliss, it's not that you *don't* hate—it's that you *can't* hate.

You can't hate anybody or anything for very long. Hate—or anything less than love—is impossible for you for very long.

Of course, this doesn't mean that blissful people will be doormats. It doesn't mean that they will be spineless.

It only means that, whatever a blissful woman does, she will do out of her bliss. She will do it from a place of love. She will do it out of her deepest sense of felt compassion.

A blissful woman's bliss only depends on her, so she will speak the loving truth. She's unconditionally blissful—there's nothing you can do to her that will change that.

She doesn't care what you think, say, or do, because her bliss is untouchable. She's completely free, and nothing you think, say, or do can take her freedom away.

In other words, when you *are* love—when you have realized your oneness with life and all life forms—"love-hate" relationships no longer exist.

There's only love, love, and more love!

TRUE LOVE IS DRAMA-FREE

Sometimes I hear people talking about the trouble that love causes,
but love—true love—never causes trouble for anybody.

Love doesn't create problems for anybody, because
love is joy, and joy is problem-free.

Love is health of the spirit, and health never causes problems for anybody.

Love doesn't create any problems for anybody—
only the ego creates problems for people.

Love never leads to misery or madness—only the loveless, joyless ego
(and its false belief in separation) leads to misery and madness.

Love born of meditation—oneness, happiness—never creates conflict and chaos.

Only love born out of the mind—separateness, unhappiness—creates drama.

Love never grows out of misery and love never leads to misery. If
your love is miserable, know one thing: It is not true love.

Love always grows out of joy and love always leads to more joy.

Love is always joyful, or it is not love at all.

•

THE CAUSE OF UNHAPPY RELATIONSHIPS

Do you know the number one cause of unhappy relationships?

The number one cause of unhappy relationships is *unhappy people*. Unhappy
relationships are caused by unhappy people searching for happiness in each other.

When you hold the belief that a relationship or another person exists to make
you happy, you are setting yourself up for the ultimate disappointment.

Instead of entering into a relationship with the hope that the other
person will make you *happy*, enter into every relationship with the
understanding that the other person will help you *grow*.

Of course, when you "grow"—when you become more
conscious—you will, inevitably, become happier, too.

RISING IN LOVE

When the individuals in a relationship understand that
the relationship exists to help them grow—and not to make
them happy—it is called a "conscious" relationship.

In an ordinary—unconscious relationship—people *shrink* spiritually;
but in a conscious relationship, people *grow* spiritually.

In a conscious relationship, when one person grows, it is reflected in the
other person—the other person grows. When the other person grows, it
is reflected back in the first person—the first person grows even more. It
is an upward spiral—higher and higher in consciousness they rise.

In other words, in ordinary love, you *fall* in love, but in divine love, you *rise* in love!

In unconscious relationships, people become *less* conscious, *less*
joyful, and *less* loving; but in conscious relationships, people
become *more* conscious, *more* joyful, and *more* loving.

The only possibility that exists for true love in a traditional context,
in the way most people mean it—"in a relationship," between two
people—is between two spiritually mature, *conscious* individuals.

If you are committed to a conscious relationship, and you can't find another
mature, conscious individual to share your spiritual journey of love with,
walk alone! That's what Buddha says, and that's what I say, too.

Please always remember: *Relationships don't exist to make you happy—relationships
exist to help you grow.* And when you grow, you inevitably become happier, too.

The art of love is finding happiness within yourself, first.

Then, when you enter into a relationship, if that is still your desire—and
see it as an opportunity to *share the happiness you already have*—you'll have
something happy, healthy, and harmonious to bring to the relationship.

You'll have something positive to share with the other.

IF I WERE YOU...

Love means understanding one thing...

If you were another person—if you were born into the same body, had the same mind, had the same upbringing, and experienced the same life circumstances as he or she has—you would think, feel, talk, and act *exactly* like he or she does.

"If I were you, I'd think, feel, talk, and act *differently*." That's *not* love.

"If I were you, I'd think, feel, talk, and act *just like you do*." That's *love*.

I can't say it enough: Love means understanding.

When you understand the cause of suffering within yourself and others— unconsciousness or unawareness—suffering ceases and joy arises automatically.

Sometimes I call this understanding "meditation."

Meditation just means looking deeply into the nature of things, so you can understand. It means looking deeply into the nature of people, so you can understand—*love*—them.

To meditate is to love.

•

LOVING YOUR ENEMIES MEANS HAVING NONE

Do you understand why people hurt each other?

Only hurting people hurt people.

When you understand this—that only hurting people hurt people—you instantly feel love for everybody, particularly people who have hurt you.

This is how you learn to love your enemies.

Of course, loving your enemies means having no enemies.

When you love your enemy, she ceases to be your enemy and instantly becomes your friend—at least in your eyes, if not her own.

TOO UNCONSCIOUS TO KNOW
THEY'RE UNCONSCIOUS

When a person is deeply unconscious, they're too unconscious to know that they're unconscious; they're not conscious enough to know that they're unconscious.

In other words, when a person is ignorant, they're too ignorant to know that they're ignorant; they're not wise enough to know that they're ignorant.

Or, said even more simply, when a person is drunk, sometimes they're too drunk to know that they're drunk; they're not sober enough to know that they're drunk.

When you understand this—that only unconscious people do hurtful, unconscious things—you no longer take things personally. You no longer take insults as insults; you no longer take attacks as attacks.

Instead, you see all "bad" behavior—all *unconscious* behavior— as a call for help, as a call for love, and as a call for deeper understanding and greater awareness on your part.

In other words, love unconscious people—they need it the most! Love unconscious people—they are great for spiritual practice.

Unconscious people allow you to deepen your consciousness.

Unconscious people are like personal trainers for the soul—for consciousness or awareness. They are personal trainers for learning— *rediscovering*—unconditional peace, love, and happiness within yourself.

YOU CAN'T BE HURT

Love is a simple understanding, a simple awareness of these truths:

"I am life itself."

"I am not my possessions."

"I am not my position."

"I am not my reputation."

"I am not my relationships.

"I am not my family, friends, or children."

"I am not my mind."

"I am nobody—"no-body," "not a body."

"I am nothing—"no-thing," "not a thing," at all.

"I am infinite, eternal life itself."

With this understanding, who and what can possibly hurt you?

Who can hurt the real you, the divine you, the you that drops this body and all this worldly, material, physical stuff at "death" and transitions to the next world, the next state of being, or the next whatever?

You, the real you—thoughtless, wordless, faceless, formless awareness itself—can't be seen, heard, or touched at all, so how can you possibly be hurt by anything or anybody?

See it:

By trying to insult you, that man is insulting himself! He's insulting no-body, no-thing. You are a transparency for the divine—his insult simply passes right through you! His insult is a projection and expression of his own awareness, not yours.

By trying to spit on you, that woman is spitting on herself! She's practically spitting on the sky—her spit is bound to return to its source. It's bound to hit her right in the face! Her spit is a projection and expression of her own consciousness, not yours.

By trying to hurt you, people are only hurting themselves! It's their own pain, suffering, and misery they are experiencing, expressing, and projecting.

They are sick, and only sickness can come from sickness.
Only vomit can come from sick people.

With this understanding, you never need to feel hurt again.

Only an unconscious person can hurt anybody and only an unconscious person can be hurt *by* anybody, in the way that I mean, because only an unconscious person is identified with form.

The conscious person is identified only with the formless—the invisible, infinite, and eternal.

This understanding—that only hurting people hurt people, that only hurting people are hurt *by* people, and that hurting people only hurt *themselves*—is love.

THE MUD AND THE LOTUS

Do you wish there was no suffering in the world? Do you
wish there was only peace, love, and happiness?

Everybody suffers.

When you understand this—that everybody suffers—you
feel love in your heart for everybody. It's automatic.

A lotus needs mud to blossom, and love needs suffering—
and an understanding of suffering—to blossom.

Love needs awareness.

In other words, with the flowering of consciousness, love goes into full bloom!

Only a person who has dived into the depths of despair can soar to the heights
of happiness. Only a person who understands the cause of suffering within
himself and others can be a source of peace, love, and happiness for the world.

Without suffering—without understanding the cause of
suffering within yourself and others—joy is not possible.

And if joy is not possible, love is not possible, either.

SUFFERING ENDS ITSELF

Unconsciousness causes suffering.

Suffering awakens consciousness.

And consciousness ends suffering.

In essence, then, suffering destroys itself.

See that? Isn't that beautiful?

It's like candle oil—it burns itself out completely and leaves no trace behind at all.

In other words, we suffer, because we are asleep.

When we suffer enough, we wake up.

When we wake up, the suffering ends.

When our suffering ends, we want to help others end their suffering, too. We want to help them do the same.

That's love.

This is why I say, "Suffering—and an understanding of suffering—leads to peace, love, and joy."

Elizabeth Kubler-Ross says it this way: "The most beautiful people we have known are those who have known defeat, known suffering, known struggle, known loss, and have found their way out of the depths. These persons have an appreciation, sensitivity, and an understanding of life that fills them with compassion, gentleness, and a deep loving concern. Beautiful people do not just happen."

I just love that.

The lotus doesn't just happen. The lotus needs the mud to blossom into something beautiful.

Likewise, true love doesn't just happen. We need suffering—and an understanding of suffering—to blossom into something truly beautiful, too.

As Jhene Aiko says, "If everything is dipped in gold, it'll never grow."

TRUE LOVE ISN'T COMPLICATED

Despite what you might have been told, love is not complicated.

Pseudo-love, need-based love, or deficient love is
complicated, because it is not love at all.

Real love is not complicated. Real love is the simplest,
most natural phenomenon there is.

A child can love; a puppy can love; a kitten can love—why not you?

If your love is complicated, it's not real love. It's lust. It's ego. It's
entertainment. It's a thousand and one things, but it's not love.

If your love is complicated, it just shows one thing: You have
yet to find happiness. You have yet to taste real joy.

You are looking for happiness in all the wrong places: worldly places. You are
searching for happiness in somebody or something else, other than yourself.

You are a beggar. You have no joy. And because you have no joy, you
have no love. Without being joyful, being loving is impossible.

As a result, you care more about *getting* love than *giving* love. You care more
about *being loved* (by others) than *being loving* (toward yourself and others).

Love is a luxury. It is always an overflow.

When you have so much joy that you can't contain it any longer and you
have to share it with the world just to unburden yourself, that's love.

Love is always about *giving* from your inner fullness, richness, and abundance.
It's never about *getting* from a place of inner emptiness, poverty, or scarcity.

Real joy is in *giving*—not just *getting*.

The real joy in life is in *loving others*—not only *being loved* by others.

Be happy, first. Love yourself, first.

Then, you can be the *source* of love!

Then, you can love others as much as you want without giving one rip
if anybody loves you back—now what is complicated about that?

TRUE LOVE IS NEVER DESTROYED

Have you ever felt that your love was "lost" or "destroyed"?

If you feel that your love has ever been lost, destroyed, or diminished, please know this: It wasn't *true* love in the first place.

It wasn't founded in joy from the jump.

It wasn't based in bliss from the beginning.

It wasn't grounded in God within from the get-go.

True love can't be destroyed or diminished. A romantic relationship may end. The love may deepen or evolve. The expression of that love may change, but the candle does not go out. The flame— the fire—continues to burn, albeit in other, purer forms.

Love is energy. Energy may change forms, but it can never be created or destroyed.

Love is never found because love is never lost.

Love is always right here where you are, no matter where you are, because you *are* love.

•

LOVE IS ITS OWN REWARD

Loving your enemies—in fact, loving anybody—is something you do for *yourself*, not for anybody else.

And, of course, that's because there is nobody else.

Or, stated differently, you *are* everybody else.

There is only One Self.

HOW LOVE FINDS YOU

People spend their whole lives looking for love, but true love is never found.

When you stop looking for love—and find fulfillment instead—*love finds you!*

People are wrong: Love doesn't lead to bliss. Bliss leads to, and is, love. Love is your bliss, overflowing. When you are really, truly blissful, your bliss explodes into love.

Love is not a duty—it is a dance!

Love is not an obligation, a responsibility, or a burden— love is a blessing and a benediction!

Love is your bliss, *shared.*

True love means being blissful. When you're blissful, you don't have to go searching for your soulmate, because everybody becomes your soulmate.

Everybody becomes another window or door through which you experience yourself—your own soul, the divine, divine bliss.

True love can't be sought. If you seek it, you will miss it.

Seeking love becomes the very obstacle to finding it.

No, nobody ever finds love. When you stop seeking love, love finds you. Love knocks at your door.

The most you can do is make yourself available to love by being at "home"—by finding peace, joy, and self-love within yourself.

Wait patiently, peacefully, and happily.

Or if you prefer, you can replace "patience" with "presence." Instead of focusing on patience, focus on presence. Instead of being patient, be present.

If you're present, you don't need to be patient.

If you can find a way to enjoy the present—your own presence, the presence of God within, Presence itself—you don't need to worry about being patient, because you are patient *already.*

Presence *is* patience.

When you are present, when you are Presence itself, there is no ego. There is no attachment to loveless, lonely thoughts. There's no addiction to unhappy, unhealthy, unharmonious thoughts.

As a result, you become an empty temple for love to enter.
You become a divine flute for divine music.

Or, more accurately, you realize that you've *always* been an empty temple
full of divine love. You've *always* been a divine flute for divine music.

If you are chasing love, please stop.

Love can't be chased because there is no way to love—love *is* the way!

Love can't be pursued because love is *in* you.

In fact, love *is* you; you are love.

Pursuing love is just chasing your own tail. Pursuing love is chasing
the wind. Just stop pursuing love, and love will pursue you.

Stop looking for love in all the wrong places: the world.

Look for love in the only place it exists: within you.

The point isn't to find love so that you can be happy some day—
the point is to be happy today so that that love can find *you!*

DON'T HELP A BEGGAR, SHARE WITH A FRIEND!

Loving people just means sharing your bliss. Helping
people just means sharing your joy.

When you're joyful, there's no ego involvement in your
help. Nobody is inferior, and nobody is superior.

When you give from a place of true love, you aren't giving
to a beggar—you're sharing with a friend!

If you want to experience true love, don't think in terms of "helping
a beggar"—think in terms of "sharing with a friend."

In other words, don't help somebody because you think you're
only doing something for him or her—you're not.

When you help somebody, you're not just doing something for him
or her—you're doing something for *yourself*, too. You're not just the
one *helping*, believe it or not—you're the one *being helped, too!*

Carl Jung writes, "Where love rules, there is no will to power, and where
power predominates, love is lacking. One is the shadow of the other."

Or as Jimi Hendrix said, "When the power of love overcomes
the love of power, the world will know peace."

Help people, but keep it pure. Don't have any ulterior motives.

Don't help because you think you will be thanked for it later—often you will not be.

Don't help because you think it will make you a better person—
it does not make you a better person, no matter what you think.
Becoming a "better" person does not come so cheaply.

Help people because you can't do otherwise. You have
so much to give that you can't contain it.

If your help is born out of your misery—out of ego, out of obligation, out of
responsibility, out of duty, or out of guilt—you're spreading misery, not joy.

Help that is born out of misery comes with a thousand and
one conditions to be met—it's greedy; it's needy.

Conditional help—like conditional love—holds everybody hostage.

You might be looking at the other as a beggar and yourself as a king, but in your misery and lack, who is really the beggar and who is really the king?

Don't give to people just because you think it is the right thing to do. Don't give to anybody only because you think giving is a good, moral, or religious thing to do—it is not.

Moralistic giving is not authentic, heartfelt, joyful giving. It is guilt-ridden giving, and guilt-ridden giving is not giving at all.

Categorically, giving is not always good. Some things should not be given. Some things we don't want.

Your misery, your expectations, your conditions, your resentment, your guilt—nobody wants these things! Don't give them to me or anybody else. Just keep them to yourself.

You can only give what you have. If you have misery, you will give misery. If you have anxiety, you will give anxiety. What good is this kind of giving?

If you really want to help people, be joyful!

Get a taste of real joy. If you are joyful, you may not be able to help people with your money, connections, or advice, but your joy will help others.

You can't help, but your joyfulness—your peaceful presence—can help. Your joyful awareness—your felt oneness with life (God) and all life forms (people)—can help.

If out of your joyfulness, you are inspired to give time, money, or anything else, all the better, but the very first requirement for genuine giving is joyfulness.

Unless your giving comes out of your joyfulness, you will not make the other person better off in the deepest, most meaningful and lasting way.

Always remember: Don't help a beggar—share with a friend!

JOYLESS LOVE ISN'T LOVE AT ALL

If you want to find love, forget about love for now and just be blissful, instead.

Love is not the highest value—*bliss* is the highest value.

Love is not the most important thing—*joy* is the most important thing.

Never put love above bliss, or you will find neither love nor bliss.

Joy is infinitely more important than love because joy is the very foundation of love. Love is simply an overflow of your joyfulness.

Bliss is the rain—love is the flood!

Bliss is the sun—love is the sunshine!

Without the rain, a flood is impossible. Without the sun, sunlight is impossible. And without joy, love can't exist.

Joy is always a higher value than love because true love is impossible without joy.

Have you noticed? There is too much joyless love in the world.

There are millions of people claiming to be deeply in love who are actually drowning in their own misery.

Joyless love is not love at all.

Joyless love is pseudo-love—only joyful love is real love.

Here's putting it another way: Joyful people are always loving people, but not all loving people—people who *claim* to be loving—are joyful people.

Without joy, love is just hot air.

When you understand love, you understand that joy is priority number one.

•

MARRIED TO BLISS

Love is a feeling of deep, inner bliss.

Love is what you feel when life becomes beautiful for no reason at all.

Love is a feeling of deep gratitude in your heart for the blessing and benediction that is life itself.

If you're looking for love, be married to bliss.

Be blissful, and love will find you.

Chapter 4

LIVE & LET LIVE

Love means accepting people for who they are, not trying
to change them into who you want them to be.

You can love people or you can try to change
them, but you can't do both.

FULFILL YOUR OWN EXPECTATIONS

Live your own life—leave everybody else and their opinions out of it.

Likewise, let everybody else live their own life—
leave yourself and your opinions out of it.

Set and fulfill your own expectations and let everybody else set and fulfill their own expectations. It's not your place to say how anybody else should live his or her life, and it's not anybody else's place to say how you should live yours.

Siddhartha didn't live to fulfill anybody else's expectations—that's how he became Buddha! He never compromised. If Buddha had lived his life to fulfill other people's expectations, he would've missed his own life, destiny, and divine purpose.

Jesus never fulfilled anybody else's expectations—that's how he became Christ! Why do you think Jesus was crucified? He was crucified because he rejected everybody else's expectations; he wouldn't compromise. Had Jesus lived his life according to other people's expectations, he would've missed his real potential. He never would've become Christ.

Never compromise yourself. Live your own life and fulfill your own expectations. Otherwise, you will never grow into your potential. Live your own life, according to your own truth, based on your own heart and soul.

You have not been put here on this earth to be imprisoned by anybody else's ideas. You've been put here on this earth with a special purpose and plan all your own—find it and fulfill it!

Likewise, permit everybody else the same freedoms you permit yourself. Never ask other people to compromise themselves. Let them live their own lives. Let them fulfill their own expectations—otherwise, how will they grow into their potential?

Don't imprison anybody. When you imprison others, you imprison yourself. To imprison others, you have to remain there in the prison with them.

Everybody has been given a divine purpose and a unique plan—help them find it and fulfill it!

Remind yourself and remind others, too: "Your only responsibility is toward your own heart. You have no responsibility toward anybody else in the world."

Don't betray yourself—that is a kind of suicide.

And don't ask anybody else to betray him or herself,
either—that is a kind of homicide.

This is my feeling: "Compromise" is an ugly word. "Compromise" means, "I give you half, you give me half, and then, each of us has half." No, that simply won't do.

Never compromise in that way. Never compromise
yourself, your life, or your happiness.

Always remember: Your expectations are your job, and everybody
else's expectations are their job. Your happiness is your responsibility,
and everybody else's happiness is their responsibility.

Don't take responsibility for how anybody else feels, and don't
blame other people for how you feel. How you feel is up to
you, and how everybody else feels is up to them.

Eleanor Roosevelt once said, "Nobody can make you
feel inferior without your own consent."

I agree. Nobody can make you feel *anything* without your own consent, and you can't make anybody else feel anything without his or her own consent, either.

LIVE AND LET LIVE

Do you want to help people?

Help them be themselves. Don't try to change them
according to your needs and desires.

Helping people is not about nailing them to posts or painting them
into corners so that you can dictate in which direction they grow.

No matter what you think—no matter how logical, reasonable, or rational
you think you are being—you don't know what anybody else really needs.

Imposing your ideas and opinions on other people does not facilitate their
growth—it stunts it. There's no freedom for anybody in dictating the direction
in which people should go or grow. Growth always requires freedom.

Contrary to what you might think, trying to change people isn't
helpful. It's not helpful to them, and it's not helpful to you.

You think that changing a person is an *opportunity* for greater
peace, love, and happiness in the *future*, but it's actually an *obstacle*
to greater peace, love, and happiness in the *present*.

In other words, don't make your peace, love, and happiness depend on
getting your way. Nobody ever gets his or her way all the time. Instead,
control the one thing, the only thing, you can control: yourself.

Life can't go your way all the time and people won't go your way all the
time, but *you* can go your way all the time, and that's what counts!

THE END OF PEOPLE-PLEASING

Love is not people-pleasing.

If you make it your job to keep anybody else in the world happy, you're training him or her to be dependent on you for their happiness.

Trying to make another person happy actually makes it less likely that they will be happy, because you are making it less likely that he or she will look for, and find, the true source of happiness within him or herself.

In other words, never give help that encourages further dependence— that is not really help. Your job is not to make people dependent on you, but to help them become *independent* of you. Your job is to help everyone get along and be happy without you.

The goal should always be to strengthen people, never to weaken people. Sometimes a helping hand strengthens, and helps most, by reaching out. Other times, a helping hand helps most by hanging back. It is always a decision that you make in the moment.

If you are trying to keep anybody else in the world happy by changing your behavior, you are preventing them from finding the source of love and happiness within themselves. You are distracting them from fulfilling their true life purpose: Self-realization, God-realization.

No matter how good you are at encouraging people to be happy and feel loved, your happiness and love never make a good substitute for their own.

Showering people with approval isn't the way—showing them the way to their own source of approval within themselves is the way.

Let everybody else off the hook, and let yourself off the hook, too: Take responsibility for your own happiness and let everybody else take responsibility for their own happiness.

PLEASE YOURSELF ALREADY

I love what Esther Hicks says: "As well-meaning as they are, most people are really more interested in you pleasing them than you pleasing yourself."

And, believe it or not, this can be a good thing.

They continue, "The biggest hypocrisy in the world is people telling you that how you feel is the most important thing to them when, in reality, how *they* feel is the most important thing to them."

Just accept that everybody is in this thing called life for him or herself, and that's a really good thing—if you understand it. It means that life is designed to lead everybody back to the only true source of love and happiness that exists in the world: themselves, the source within themselves, the God within themselves.

Your purpose isn't to make anybody else in the world happy—your purpose is to make *yourself* happy.

Your purpose, like mine, is to teach people, through the clarity of your living example, how to be peaceful, loving, and happy, regardless of conditions.

•

CELEBRATE THE WORLD

Don't fight the world.

By fighting the world, you become like the world. You become just like the people you are fighting against.

To totally transform the world, don't fight—love!

Don't be like "them." Don't be a part of the problem—be a part of the solution.

If the world is suffering and fighting, and you are suffering and fighting, you cannot do anything about the world's suffering and fighting until you stop becoming part of the problem. You are not really helping until you become part of the solution.

In one lifetime, you can't totally transform the world, but you can enjoy it. You can love it.

Don't waste your life fighting and struggling—celebrate, instead!

We can change the world, but it will happen through celebration. It will happen through dance, song, music, meditation, and love—not struggle.

SAVING THE WORLD

If you think you need to save the world before you
can be happy, you're part of the problem.

Instead, be a part of the solution: Get happy and, in your
happiness, you will have something to give others.

Nobody needs to be saved because no souls are lost. All souls are home
already. All souls are home in—at one with—life (God) already.

All souls are home in love already—they just don't
know it. Remind them maybe, that's all.

There is nothing but life, so if any soul is lost, it is lost in life. There is nothing
but love—oneness with life—so if any soul is lost, it is lost in love.

We live in an ocean of love because we live in an ocean of life.

Love is not a mission to save souls—love is a mission to celebrate life!

Love isn't about salvation—love is about celebration!

Through your celebration, you will inspire others to be authentically happy.
And when they're authentically happy, they'll be authentically loving, too.

The world is alright. It's not going to hell in a handbasket—it's on the way to heaven.

In fact, we are all in heaven already, and heaven is *in*
us already—we just don't all know it yet.

When the world is ready for peace, love, and happiness, it
will have peace, love, and happiness. It's that simple.

More accurately, when any *individual* is ready for peace, love, and
happiness, she will have peace, love, and happiness. By virtue of her
awareness, she will find herself living in peace, love, and happiness,
despite the apparent chaos, confusion, and conflict in the world.

Peace, love, and happiness are always where we are, no matter where we
are. It's just that we each, individually, have to open our eyes to see it.

I can't do it for you, and you can't do it for me. Only I can see through my eyes,
and only you can see through your eyes. We each have to do it for ourselves.

And when we do it for ourselves, we are doing it for everybody
in the world, too, even if they don't know it.

TO HELP, BE HAPPY

This will sound contradictory at first, but it is not.

The world is never going to be peaceful, loving, or happy.

It has never been so, and it is never going to be so. The world can't be peaceful, loving, or happy, because only *individuals* can be peaceful, loving, and happy.

Peace, love, and happiness are personal.

The only real help you can offer the world is your
unconditional peace, love, and happiness.

When you are peaceful, loving, and happy, the world is more peaceful, loving, and happy, too, because you are a significant part of the world. You are the closest thing to the world, so when you change, the world changes.

If you want to live in a more peaceful, loving, and happy
world, be more peaceful, loving, and happy yourself.

Don't try to fix the world—instead, overcome it
by being peaceful, loving, and happy!

The world doesn't need to be fixed. Even if it needed to be fixed, it can't be fixed. Even if it could be fixed, you couldn't fix it. If Buddha couldn't do it, if Jesus couldn't do it, if Lao Tzu couldn't do it, what makes you think you could do it?

Don't try to save anybody else. Everybody must save themself. In
the end, everybody saves themself or is not saved at all.

As Byron Katie says, "You can tell the story about how you helped somebody find their way, but ultimately, everybody finds their own way."

If you really want to help people, get out of their way.

Understand me: I'm not saying not to help people.

I'm saying that unless people are asking for your help, they aren't ready to receive it—that's what I'm saying. If they aren't asking, there is no wanting. And without wanting, your words will just fall on deaf ears.

Believe it or not, as Byron Katie says, "All the advice you've ever given anybody else was actually meant for you. Go inside and see how this is true."

Don't try to save anybody else—save yourself. That's enough, more than enough.

Saving yourself (from unhappiness) is an act of infinite love and kindness, because when you save yourself (from unhappiness), you save the world from a thousand and one problems you would have otherwise created through your unhappiness.

GET OUT OF MY SUNLIGHT

Sometimes I go sunbathing.

I love sunbathing. When I'm sunbathing, I'm happy. I'm perfectly content. Everything is just perfect.

Inevitably, of course, somebody stands directly in my sunlight and, then, proceeds to ask me how they can help me.

"Just get out of my way! Just get out of my sunlight already! That's all the help I need. Just leave me alone!" Ha!

I'm exaggerating *a lot*, but isn't that the response you get from people when you try to offer your unsolicited advice to them?

"Just leave me alone already!" Ha!

Don't worry: Everybody finds their own way.

If and when they ask, support them and help them to discover their own path and take their own journey, but don't try to change anybody according to your ideas. Just help them be themselves.

Live, love, and let go.

If you really want to help people, don't treat them like you want to be treated. Treat them like *they* want to be treated. Often, that means leaving them alone.

Love people enough to stay out of their business. Don't think about what other people are doing. Just live your life as well as you can, as blissfully as you can, and share your bliss with them.

Even having an opinion about another person's life is often interfering in it. Don't even have an opinion about other people. To be really blissful means to be non-interfering. It means not having an opinion about anybody at all.

Buddha says, "People with opinions just go around bothering people."

Who are you to even have an opinion about somebody else?

BE YOURSELF: BE LOVE!

To help the world, be yourself.

Be your true Self. Be your peaceful, loving, joyful Self.

Believe it or not, sometimes not doing anything and just being
yourself is more helpful than doing anything in particular.
Sometimes just being yourself—not fixing, changing, talking, or
teaching—can change a situation in a way nothing else can.

People don't need your logic—they need your love.

People don't need your advice—they need your loving awareness.

Besides, words don't teach anyway—only life experience teaches. Everybody
must learn from their own life experience. There really is no other way.

Besides, who are you to decide what is right for anybody else? Unless
they are asking for it, it is none of your business to advise the world.

To help the world, be more loving; be more accepting.

Show people that you can be peaceful, loving, and joyful
whenever you want, regardless of what is happening around
you, regardless of what everybody else is doing.

Let everybody know—through your living, shining example—that you don't hold
anybody else responsible for your peace, love, and happiness, and that they don't
need to make anybody else responsible for their peace, love, and happiness, either.

Just be a peaceful, loving, happy presence in the world.

Unless people explicitly request it, don't give advice; don't provide
counsel. If you want to make recommendations or suggestions, please
ask them if they want your recommendations or suggestions first.

In other words, keep your nose out of other people's business. If they are doing
something wrong, that's for them to realize. Nobody else can make them realize it.

Until they realize it, your words are falling on deaf ears. You're wasting
your valuable time and energy explaining the inexplicable, trying to
get them to understand what they can't quite yet understand.

Of course, once they realize it, your words will be falling on even deafer ears. You're
wasting your precious time and energy explaining what is already understood.

Always remember: A wise person never gives unsolicited advice, because a wise person knows that the only thing freely given—and never taken—is unsolicited advice.

So, please, never try to convince or persuade anybody to your way of thinking using reason, logic, or argument.

Remember: "A person convinced against their will is of the same opinion still."
—Samuel Butler, English poet

Just be happy.

When you're happy, you'll be loving. If you can be loving— if you can be love itself—the situation can change.

Love changes things.

In fact, love is the *only* thing that ever does change things. Love is the only truly transformative power in the world.

In the end, love—true love, divine love—conquers all.

THE SOURCE OF ALL SORROW

Judgment destroys joy.

Judgment is the source of all sorrow.

Judgment doesn't just hurt others—judgment hurts
you, the self-appointed judge, too.

When you're judgmental, you're not joyful. And when
you're not joyful, you can't be loving.

Love, which is joy, is really just one thing: non-judgment.

Don't judge—everybody is doing the best they can.
When people know better, they'll do better.

So, let up, lighten up, and leave people alone.

You don't know enough about anybody or anything to judge
them. All judgments are half-baked opinions.

Don't judge other people's behavior—just seek your own happiness within.

•

TRUE EMPATHY

True empathy is staying focused on the formless, not form.

It's staying focused on the spiritual, not the physical.

It's staying focused on the infinite, eternal, formless essence—
not the finite, temporal, ephemeral forms.

It's staying focused on truth, not illusion.

It's staying focused on God, the God within yourself
and all people, not people themselves.

It's staying focused on the One Presence within
all people, not the people themselves.

It's staying on the side of peace, love, and joy.

RAISING CONSCIOUSNESS

Your desire to help always needs to be balanced with an understanding of the impermanence of form, the eternal nature of all life, and the ultimate illusion of all pain.

With that understanding, love will flow into and out of everything you do. The whole world will be benefited.

In other words, true change happens within, not without.

Make the causal level—consciousness—your primary focus.

Make teaching enlightenment—peaceful, loving, joyful presence one moment at a time—your main purpose.

Make your own peaceful, loving, joyful presence your gift to the world.

Who—and *what*—you are is always infinitely more powerful than anything you can think, say, or do.

Please understand me: That does not mean that you shouldn't take action. No, just the contrary: Take action! Take action if you want, but let your action be inspired from your presence, from Presence itself—from peace, love, and joy.

People think that by changing things—external circumstances, other people, the government, the economy, the educational system, or whatever—they can change the world. However, you cannot change the world simply by changing things, because unless consciousness is changed, there will always be more problems—in fact, bigger problems—in the world.

The same consciousness that created the original problems will simply create more and more—bigger and bigger—problems.

Unless consciousness is changed, nothing is changed. Until consciousness is raised, nothing is really ever improved.

SAVE YOURSELF

Ignorant people spend their whole lives trying to change the world or other people, but wise people focus primarily on changing themselves.

When your consciousness is raised, the entire world's consciousness is raised without any additional effort.

Like the light that flows from a lamp or like the fragrance that flows from a flower, help flows from you effortlessly.

Enlighten the world by enlightening yourself. Raise the world's consciousness by raising your own.

Stay centered in the unchanging watcher that is at the center of your being. Learn to see life from a broader perspective—through Source's eyes, through Love's eyes.

Through nonjudgmental awareness.

Happiness comes and goes; misery comes and goes; success comes and goes; failure comes and goes. Everything comes and goes, except one thing: nonjudgmental awareness.

Stay centered in love—nonjudgmental, non-clinging awareness—and everything will become a passing phenomenon. Don't cling to any moment because it's beautiful, and don't push away any moment because it's ugly.

This is called "enlightenment."

It's called "peace," "love," and "happiness."

It's also called "sanity."

Become enlightened—that's how you save the world.

Your enlightenment is your gift to the world. Become enlightened and, then, go share your enlightenment with the world.

Here's another way of saying it: To become enlightened, simply decide to be unconditionally happy for the rest of your life. Then, you will not only become unconditionally happy; you will become enlightened, too.

That's what Michael Singer says, and I agree.

Learning to become unconditionally happy is the spiritual path that ultimately leads you—and the rest of the world, one individual at a time—to enlightenment.

ENJOY PEOPLE

If you can learn to be unconditionally happy, you will be people's greatest help.

If you are trying to change people or the world, you can't be joyful, because joy is about *enjoying* people and the world, *not changing them.*

The only way to be joyful—and change people, too—is to enjoy them, to love them. To change others, give up wanting to change others and just enjoy and love them, instead.

If you want others to transform, you're not fully transformed—come back home. Work on your own transformation first.

If you have a single complaint or gripe, you're not yet ready. You still don't understand. Your awareness isn't yet ripe enough. You're still unprepared.

If you have any remnant of unhappiness left inside, you have not yet graduated. Your house is not in order. Something in your understanding is still missing.

Get your house in order, first, before you go out into the world and create more problems for everybody.

•

ENJOYMENT OVER IMPROVEMENT

Stop trying to always improve life.

It's fine to improve your life conditions—the quality of your life—but improving life itself is impossible.

Life—the life within you (God)—is sacred. It can't be improved.

If you try to improve it, you will ruin (your experience of) it, no matter what you do. This is what Lao Tzu says, and this is what I say, too.

Instead, learn to love life. Learn to enjoy life—the silent, sacred life within you, the peaceful aliveness inside you—the best you can.

The best way to change life without is to love life within. The best way to change outer conditions is by loving inner consciousness.

Sometimes people call this "meditation," "prayer," or "practicing the presence of God within."

I just call it "love."

LOVE ISN'T SUFFERING

Let me debunk this myth right now:

You don't have to suffer to be kind to the world. You don't
have to suffer with the world to help the world.

In fact, if you are suffering with the world, you can't help the
world. If you are drowning, you can't save anybody else from
drowning. Please understand this simple thing.

Misery loves company, but you can't help your company if you are miserable.

It's only by finding the right path that you can share that path
with others. It's only by transcending your own suffering that
you can help others transcend their suffering, too.

So, please don't empathize too much with anybody's suffering.

Empathize with the *person*, but don't empathize too much with their *pain*.
Remember, you can't feel anybody else's pain—you can only feel your *own*.

You can only experience the suffering you create for yourself as a result of
the thoughts you think in *your* head. You can only feel your own pain—the
pain you create for yourself—by imagining the pain that other people feel.
In other words, you always suffer from *your own* thoughts and feelings.

Plus, your suffering doesn't relieve other people of
their suffering. It doesn't help them at all.

Seeing the weakness and suffering in people isn't the best way to help
them. Yes, be present with them, listen to them, and understand them.
Yes, be there for them, but do not let your light be dimmed. Do not let
your enlightenment be diminished. Do not let your bliss burn out.

That's what I mean by, "Empathize with people, but
don't empathize too much with their pain."

Empathize with people, but not too much with their pain, or their pain will
become your pain, figuratively and literally. Before you know it, you will be
suffering the same thoughts, feelings, and experiences they are suffering.

People who are suffering don't need your suffering—they have enough of their own!

People who are suffering don't need more unhappiness—
they need more peace, love, and joy!

Helping people doesn't mean giving them more of what they already have but don't want (unhappiness)—helping people means giving them what they *don't* (know they) already have and need more of (happiness).

If you allow your light to be dimmed by people who are suffering or by people who are causing suffering, how can you possibly show anybody the way?

If you allow your candle to be blown out by anything, how can you be a light to anybody?

How can you, in your darkness, show other people, who are also living in darkness, the path out of darkness?

You're helpless—how can you be helpful?

You're lost—how can you show the way?

You're blind—how can you lead the blind?

No, you have to remain a light. You have to remain lit up—peaceful, loving, and joyful—if you want to show people the path. There is no other way.

You can do it—you can remain lit up, no matter what.

Buddha says, "There isn't enough darkness in all the world to snuff out the light of one little candle."

You are that one little candle—the world needs that light, *your* light, not more darkness!

So, please don't think that loving people or helping people ever means suffering with them, no matter how seemingly noble the cause. It does not mean that.

No matter what you think, you can't ever feel another person's pain—you can only feel *your own.*

No matter what people tell you, you never help anybody by hiding your light under a bushel, by "suffering" with him or her.

Love them—and yourself—instead!

BE A LIGHTHOUSE

Your purpose is to wake up and help others wake up through your living example.

Your purpose in life is to wake up to the innate peace, love, and happiness within yourself and help others wake up to the innate peace, love, and joy within them.

When you are motivated to wake up—and help others wake up through your living, shining example—you have so much peace, love, and joy that nothing else can compare.

As it's said, "The world doesn't need to hear another sermon nearly as much as it needs to see one."

Preach without preaching: Turn everything you do into a living sermon by doing it with real peace, love, and joy.

Benjamin Franklin is right, "Lighthouses [can sometimes] be more helpful than churches."

That's because lighthouses don't go looking for boats to save—they just stand there shining.

If you want to be a light to the world, stay "home"—remain peaceful, loving, and joyful—and keep your own candle lit.

The moment you leave home—the moment you lose your peace, joy, and love and start taking on the world's misery—is the moment your candle goes out.

You can only be a light to the world if you remain lit up.

That's what enlightenment means: being "lit up," being a lighthouse for the world.

BE A WELL

Being blissful—and, therefore, loving—is like being a well.

A well doesn't go looking for people who are thirsty in order to quench their thirst—*people* who are thirsty go looking for a well in order to quench their own thirst. A well just makes itself available, infinitely available, to those who are thirsty.

If you're thirsty, you have to go to the well to quench your thirst—the well is not going to come to you!

When you are blissful, you don't need to find people to help. Wherever you are, wherever you find yourself, your very being is helpful without doing anything else on your part. If you sit next to a tree, your very presence helps the tree without any effort on your part.

A real master never seeks people to change them— people seek the master to change *themselves*!

That's why they are called "seekers," and she is called "the master."

Masters are just like a pool of cold water. Thirsty people come to it—it doesn't go to people.

Just change yourself.

If you are able to change yourself, that is enough. That is more than enough. Everything else will begin to happen on its own accord.

Witnessing your transformation, people around you will want to know your secret. Seeing your change, people around you will begin changing, too.

Spiritual transformation is contagious, highly contagious!

Presence is inflammatory, highly inflammatory!

When you change, others change. When you change, the world changes. When you become a light, before long, the entire world around you is on fire!

Give up helping people who haven't asked for your help, and you will be people's greatest help.

JUST ACCEPT PEOPLE

Let me be clear: I'm not saying that people don't change.

People do change... sometimes.

When people change, however, they do so according to themselves, according to their own needs and desires. They change in their own direction and in their own timing, not yours.

People change when *they* are willing and ready to change, not when *you* are willing and ready for them to change.

In fact, external pressure from others usually only prevents people from changing. When people change out of utter, outer obligation—for extrinsic reasons and not for intrinsic reasons—that change never lasts long.

Plus, forcing people to change only creates bitterness and resentment. It doesn't work.

Don't make your peace, love, and happiness contingent on people doing what you want. People do what *they* want, not what *you* want.

And usually, the more you push people to do things your way, the more those people push back. The more you insist people do things your way, the more those people insist on doing things their own way just to declare their freedom and independence.

Don't you do the same thing?

Rilke puts it beautifully. He says, "Once the realization is accepted that even between the closest human beings infinite distances continue, a wonderful living side by side can grow, if they succeed in loving the distance between them which makes it possible for each to see the other whole against the sky."

You can't change anybody. All you can do is create a little sacred space for change to happen, for grace to enter. Through your unconditional acceptance, you can create a little temple inside yourself and inside the relationship for love to do its miracle work. That's the most you can do.

The truth is that when you accept people as they are, only then do they change.

When you drop your expectations of what life should be, happiness happens; and when you drop your insistence upon what people should be, love happens.

Rigid expectations always lead to unhappiness, and
unhappiness always hurts your love life.

Drop your rigid expectations—then, everything that happens will fulfill you.

UNCONDITIONAL ACCEPTANCE

The guiding principle for all happy relationships is just this:

Drop your expectations and completely accept people for who they are.

When it comes to relationships, acceptance is the only
rule; non-judgment is the only principle.

When you are nonjudgmental, you are love already.

Accept people for who they are right now, not for who they might become later.

There's nothing more damaging to a relationship than trying to
change the other person, and there's nothing more transformative
for a relationship than completely accepting the other person.

If you can't do that—if you can't accept him or her for
who they are—do everybody a favor: move on!

When you accept people as they are, you don't have to exert
extra effort to love them. You love them already.

Acceptance—joyful acceptance, not reluctant
acceptance—is love. It is unconditional love.

Love the person, and forget about the future—the future is uncertain.

When you accept people for who they are, you'll be happy with them no matter
what. If they do change in a "positive" way, you'll be pleasantly surprised. If they
don't change or they change in a "negative" way, you won't be disappointed.

Never wait for anybody or anything to change before you get happy, because if you
miss an opportunity to be happy, you miss an opportunity to experience love, too.

Remember, true love is unconditional happiness, and
unconditional happiness is true love.

The only way to be unconditionally loving is to be unconditionally happy, and
the only way to be unconditionally happy is to be unconditionally loving.

Of course, I'm not telling you to stay in a relationship if you are
unhappy. Sometimes you have to love people from a distance.
Loving people doesn't mean that you have to be in a romantic
relationship—or relationship of any kind—with them.

If you want to be unconditionally happy, you have to make your experience of peace, love, and happiness depend on you and you only.

You can control yourself, but you can't control anybody else. It's not within your power—nor is it your pleasure or privilege—to control other people.

Remember, it takes two to tango and two to fight, but it only takes one person to be happy and in love. And that one person is you!

You're the one you've been waiting for your whole life.
The soulmate you've been searching for is *you*.

BE A DROPOUT!

Be a dropout!

By "Be a dropout," I don't mean what you think I mean.

I don't mean to leave the world.

I don't mean to drop out of society.

Be in the world and live in society, but drop the world and leave society *out of you.*

Be in the world but not *of* it.

Live in the world, but don't let the world live in *you.*

Live in the crazy, chaotic, confused world, but don't let the crazy, chaotic, confused thinking and ways of the world live in you.

That's what I'm saying.

●

LOVE IS NOT WORRYING

You can't worry about people and love them at the same time.

You can do one or the other—love them *or* worry about them—but you can't do both, simultaneously.

If you are busy worrying about somebody, you can't also be loving them at the same time. If you are busy loving them, you can't also be worried about them, simultaneously.

Worry is fear, and fear is the absence of love.

Buddha says, "The whole secret of existence is to have no fear."

The whole secret of existence is not to worry!

Worry less—*live* more!

Worry less—*love* more!

Worry less—*enjoy* more!

FREE LOVE

Life is not going to follow you—you must follow life.

Life is not going to listen to you—you must listen to life.

Everything and everybody in life is not going to go
your way, so it's up to you to go your way.

If life isn't going your way, isn't it even more important for you to go your way?

If you can't control life, isn't it even more critical to control the one thing
that you *can* control, the one thing that is in your hands: *yourself.*

You can't force life to flow according to you. Life does what it
wants, whether you want it to or not—love life anyway.

Likewise, people do what they want, despite what you
want them to do—love them anyway.

Try it for twenty-four hours: Flow with everything. Feel grateful
for whatever life gives you. Maintain a graceful, grateful
attitude all day. Keep an appreciative attitude all night.

You'll be surprised: With a non-attached, nonjudgmental attitude, you'll find love
everywhere. You'll find the extraordinary hiding in the most ordinary places.

You'll find love hiding in the most unlikely places and most "unlovable" people.

THIS, TOO, SHALL PASS

To love, let go of your attachments.

Let go of your attachments to everybody and everything
being a certain way... or being—existing—at all.

To let go of your attachments, just become aware of them. By becoming
aware of them, your attachments will drop by themselves.

By nonjudgmentally observing your attachments, you begin to
understand the futility of your attachments—that's what I mean.

Then, your attachments are no longer problems for you.

The way out of attachment is through awareness, and
awareness is sometimes called "meditation."

Meditation is nothing serious. It's nothing complicated. Meditation just means
watching the changing nature of all things from a place of unchanging awareness.

It just means watching the tide of life go out and come back in. It just means
watching the waves of life—thoughts, feelings, circumstances, and people—rise
and fall, ebb and flow, build and crash on the seashore of life, over and over again.

When you become aware of the impermanent and changing nature
of all things, nothing disturbs your peace the way it used to. You stop
identifying with things that change, and you start identifying with that
which never changes: Awareness, Consciousness, or Presence itself.

When you look at the impermanent, passing phenomenon of life from
the perspective of unchanging, eternal awareness, you are looking at life
through Source's eyes, through God's eyes, through Love's eyes.

When you look at life in this unattached, non-judgmental way,
you are looking at life with compassionate, loving eyes.

"This, too, shall pass"—that's the highest perspective.

And "this" includes all internal and external conditions. All people,
places, and things. All conditions, circumstances and experiences.
All thoughts, feelings, sensations, and perceptions.

By noticing our attachments without judgment, we render those
attachments powerless. The bonds that bind us are broken.

Not that we break those bonds, mind you, but the bonds are broken, nonetheless. The non-attachment, the non-identification, the non-judgment—Awareness, Consciousness, Presence—does the work.

Love—nonjudgmental awareness—does the work!

When you are aware—when you are Awareness itself—you are not attached or identified with anything whatsoever. You observe it all and accept it all, without judgment.

That unattached, unidentified, divine Awareness is love.

Chapter 5

SELF-LOVE

Love starts with self-love.

To properly love others, you have to love yourself.

When you love yourself, you automatically start loving others.

SELFISH OR UNSELFISH?

Being happy is simultaneously the most selfish and
least selfish thing you can do in the world.

In other words, it takes an authentically selfish person to be authentically unselfish.

It sounds counter-intuitive, but it's true: You have to *get* it
to *give* it. You have to *have* it before you can *share* it.

Selfishness is at the very core of my teaching, because unless you are selfish enough
to find happiness within yourself, you have nothing to give anybody else anyway.

Unless you are selfish enough—self-loving enough, self-aware enough—
to be happy, you have nothing to share with anybody else.

•

YOUR FIRST LOVE

If you really want a relationship with somebody else, make the relationship
you have with yourself the most important relationship of all.

If you do that, all of your other relationships will fall neatly into place.

Of course, "neatly into place" doesn't mean they will always
be "perfect" from your limited, human perspective.

"Neatly into place" means you will find harmony with others, even when they
don't find harmony with you. You will be able to find peace, love, and happiness
within yourself, even when other people don't do what you want them to do.

When you put your relationship with yourself first, nothing
can disturb your peace, love, and happiness any longer.

And isn't that the point of it all anyway?

TRUE COMMITMENT

Contrary to popular belief, there is a bigger problem than a person not committing to you and that is a person not committing to *him or herself*, first.

Not committing to his own spiritual awakening.

Not committing to her own spiritual growth.

Not committing to his own relationship with God within.

Not committing to her own alignment with Source.

Not committing to his own connectedness with Being.

Not committing to her own peace, love, and joy.

Not committing to loving him or herself, first and foremost.

When the foundation is built on shifting sand, the entire building is bound to fall. When you don't commit to yourself first, any commitment you make to anybody else is false and bound to fail.

•

GO AHEAD: LOVE YOURSELF!

So many people have the wrong idea about self-love.

They think that loving yourself is arrogant, but loving yourself is not arrogant.

Self-love is really life-love; self-love is really God-love.

By loving yourself in the way that I mean it, you are loving who and what you really are at the formless level: life itself (God).

Life is the painter, and you are the painting—the credit goes not to the painter, but the painting.

God is the sculptor, and you are the sculpture—the credit belongs to the sculptor, not the sculpture.

The real credit goes to the creator, not the creation.

The real credit belongs to life itself (God)—not you, not the ego that you think is you.

So, go ahead: For life's sake—for God's sake—love yourself.

Love yourself—your true, infinite, eternal Self.

THE DANCE, THE DANCER, AND THE DANCED

Life is inside you.

In fact, you *are* life.

Life is the painter, and you are the painting. The painter pours himself into the painting. In the painting, the painter and the painted are not two—they are one.

Life is the dancer, and you are the dance. The dancer dissolves herself into the dance. In the dance, the dancer and the danced are not two—they are one.

When you love yourself in the way that I mean it, the lover is dissolved into the loved. The lover is merged with the beloved. There are not two energies—there is just one.

When you love yourself in the way that I mean, you have come to realize that you, life, and all life forms are one.

•

ACCEPT YOURSELF TO ACCEPT OTHERS

When you start accepting yourself, the real miracle happens:

You start accepting others, too.

And when you start accepting others—without judgment, criticism, or condemnation—the possibility of true love finally becomes real for you.

When you really accept yourself, your heart starts beating with gratitude; it starts throbbing with heartfelt appreciation. That unaddressed gratitude is true love.

Unaddressed love is the ultimate experience. It is the greatest blessing and benediction that can happen in your life.

Accept and love yourself, and you will come to accept and love others, too.

All acceptance starts with self-acceptance; all love starts with self-love.

LOVE YOURSELF TO LOVE OTHERS

Do you think loving yourself is something you do only, or primarily, for yourself? Do you think loving yourself is something that only benefits you?

No, loving yourself is something you do for the world, too!

Unless you love yourself, you cannot love other people. When you start loving yourself, you finally become capable of loving others.

Loving yourself is the first and only requirement for loving other people.

Love yourself—you owe that much to the world!

Remember: Self-love is simultaneously the most selfish and least selfish thing you can do in the world.

Let me explain. Unless you love yourself, you cannot love anybody else, because you have nothing to give anybody else.

But also, unless you love other people, you have not sufficiently loved yourself. Loving other people is proof that you have successfully loved yourself. Authentically and unconditionally loving others is evidence of your self-love.

Loving yourself is not selfish—only people who *don't* love themselves are truly selfish.

Loving yourself is not irresponsible—loving yourself is the *most responsible* thing you can do for yourself, your friends, your family, your enemies, and the world as a whole.

If you don't love yourself, you're full of poison and sickness. When you're full of poison, only poison can come from you; when you're full of sickness, only sickness can come from you.

How can you love anybody if you are full of hate?

You can only share what you have. Loving others is impossible unless you are full of love for yourself.

Always remember: It takes an authentically *selfish* person to be authentically *unselfish*.

Buddha says, "You can search throughout the entire universe for someone who is more deserving of your love and affection than you are yourself, and that person is not to be found anywhere. You yourself, as much as anybody in the entire universe, deserves your love and affection."

LOVE YOURSELF TO BE LOVED BY OTHERS

If you don't love yourself, you can't love anybody else,
and nobody else can love you, either.

If you don't love yourself, you can't give love, and you can't receive love, either.

Without self-love, *you can't experience love at all!*

If you don't love yourself, you won't feel loved by anybody else, no matter
how much love they show you. No matter what anybody else says or does,
you won't ever feel truly loved, accepted, or appreciated by anybody.

Unless you love yourself, your heart isn't open. And without an open
heart, you can't let love in. You're a "hungry ghost." A hungry ghost is
someone who is searching for love but incapable of receiving it.

In other words, if you don't love yourself, you won't be able to
accept anybody else's love. If somebody loves you, you won't
believe him. You won't trust her. You'll always doubt their motives,
intentions, or faithfulness. You'll always doubt their love.

"I know myself. I know myself better than anybody else. How could he love me?
I'm ugly! I'm stupid! How could he find me beautiful, intelligent, or attractive?"

When you don't love yourself, you are in hell, and nobody can bring you out but
you. Even if somebody comes along and says you are beautiful, you won't trust
him. You'll think he's trying to cheat you, exploit you, or get something from you.

"How can I be beautiful? I know myself better than he knows me. I'm
not beautiful. I'm ugly. I'm the ugliest person in the world!"

If you don't love yourself, you'll go out of your way to prove you're not worth
loving. You won't stop until you prove yourself right. You won't stop until your
partner corroborates your story and confirms your negative self-concept.

Often, this means you won't stop until your partner leaves you, your boss
fires you, your friend unfriends you, or your family disowns you.

No, if you want to find love—if you want to be capable of
both giving and receiving love—love yourself.

Love yourself, and then *other people* will be able to love you.

Love yourself, and *you* will be able to love other people, too.

THE GIVING TREE

Do you consider a tree selfish?

A tree absorbs all the sunlight, water, and nutrients it possibly can. It takes up as much space as it can. It drives its roots deep into the earth, and it sends its branches, leaves, and flowers high into the sky.

Then, it blossoms. It produces fruit. It shades the flora and fauna beneath it on the ground below. It provides fresh, clean oxygen to the world. It prevents erosion of the soil so that other plants can make a home there, too. It gives shelter to animals. It provides a home for birds and their bird families. It fills the air with a fruity fragrance.

Do you call that selfish?

What if a tree gave before it was ready? What if a tree gave "unselfishly" or "altruistically"? What if it didn't absorb the water it needed? What if it didn't absorb the nutrients it needed? What if it didn't claim the sunshine it needed? What if it didn't take up the space it needed to grow and flourish? What if it didn't drive its roots deep into the earth? What if it didn't extend its branches high into the sky? Then, what would happen to all of the other life that depended on that tree for food and shelter?

Have you ever read Shel Silverstein's children's book, *The Giving Tree*? *The Giving Tree* is a story about a tree that befriends a boy. The tree gives and gives and never gets. Before long, the "poor" tree has nothing left to give.

In the world, people call that "love," but that's not love. That's martyrdom, that's masochism. That's anything but love—that's *anti*-love.

No, get first, and then give.

Get so that you have something to give. Go to the source of love, first—the source within you, the source that *is* you—so that you have something of real value and meaning to share with the world.

Your first responsibility is always toward yourself—everything else comes second.

Being self-centered—centered in your spiritual Self, grounded in God within—is the only truly happy, loving way to live.

You are the center of your universe, so to speak; your world revolves around you. Unless you are solid and stable, how can you expect to feel at home in the world?

Be for yourself, or nobody will be for you. Love yourself, or nobody will love you.

But don't only be for yourself. Don't only love yourself.

Be for other people, too. Love other people, too, or your life
will be meaningless. Only love gives life meaning.

Be for yourself, and be for others, also! Love yourself, and love other people, too!

Then your life will be meaningful, too.

IT TAKES LOVE TO RECOGNIZE LOVE

Unless you *are* love—unless you are self-loving, unless you are selfish enough to be joyful—it is impossible to know what real love is.

Unless you are love, you might think you know what love *should be*, but you won't know what love *actually is*. Unless you are spiritually awake—and your eyes are open—it is impossible to see the difference between real love and what the world thinks is love.

Unless you are love, it is impossible to discern between what grows out of love and what grows out of the ego; what grows out of joy and what grows out of misery; what is born out of fullness and fulfillment and what is born out of emptiness and unhappiness.

It takes like to recognize like; light to recognize light; and love to recognize love!

It takes a genius to recognize a genius. It takes almost a Mozart to recognize a Mozart. And the more subtle the work, the more difficult it is to find somebody to recognize it.

Living in the valley, you cannot recognize a Buddha or a Jesus—they will look like regular men to you. To recognize Buddha, you have to be almost on Buddha's level. To recognize Jesus, you have to practically be on Jesus' level.

Most people can't recognize or fully appreciate a superstar, spiritual or otherwise. They can't see the difference between pseudo, need-based love and real, joy-based love.

To recognize love, you have to *be* love. You have to be self-loving; you have to be joyful already!

I'm sorry—there is no other way.

I DON'T NEED YOUR LOVE

The truth is hard to hear, but it needs to be heard, nonetheless:

It's only once your *need to be needed* has disappeared that you are free to love anybody else. It's only once your *need to be loved* has disappeared completely from your life that you are ready to love anybody else.

It's not hard.

When you look deeply, you can easily see the futility of seeking approval and acceptance from other people. Then, your need to be needed—your deficit-based, need-based, pseudo-love—dies a natural death. It falls away on its own dead weight.

When you no longer need to be loved by anybody else, I call that "self-love." I call that the beginning of true love or divine love. When your need to be loved has disappeared completely, only then are you really ready for love.

We all worry too much about whether other people like us or not. We all worry too much about whether other people love us or not.

Who cares if anybody loves you—that's *your* job!

Who cares if anybody likes you—that's *your* responsibility!

Do *you* like you? That's what matters.

Do *you* love you? That's what counts.

If you don't love yourself, nobody and nothing else can ever make you feel loved for long.

Please remember this simple thing.

UNCONDITIONAL SELF-LOVE

Lots of people talk about wanting unconditional love, but then they turn right back around and attach conditions to their love for themselves.

Love yourself despite the extra pounds, the too few dollars, the lack of a partner, or whatever.

Of course, that doesn't mean that you can't or shouldn't make changes in your life. If you want to—and can—improve your life situation, improve it. If you don't want to—or can't—improve your life situation, don't improve it. That's not what I'm saying.

I'm simply saying this: Don't wait until you—or your "life"— are perfect before you start loving yourself.

If you wait until you are perfect before you start loving yourself, you'll wait an entire lifetime. If you wait until your life circumstances are perfect before you start loving yourself, you'll never love yourself, and you'll never experience true love.

However, if you start loving yourself before everything is perfect, you'll find that everything is *already* perfect. It's a miracle of miracles.

Self-love isn't about creating a perfect life or a perfect you so that you can love yourself.

Self-love is about loving yourself (and your life) right now, no matter what, so that you can discover the perfection that already exists within you (and your life) already.

In other words, never wait for anybody or anything to change, including yourself, before you get happy. Don't attach even a single condition to your happiness or self-love.

Self-love is not earned—it is *accepted*!

Self-love is not a reward—it is a *realization*!

Self-love is a choice.

We each set the bar for ourselves, so why not set the bar low? Better yet, why not remove the bar altogether? Why do you need even one requirement or condition for experiencing peace, love, and happiness? Why purposely put even a single obstacle in your own way?

Attaching conditions to your self-love and happiness is like running an imaginary race against imaginary competitors and intentionally placing hurdles in the way. Now, does that make sense at all?

Love yourself unconditionally, and then you can jump as high as you want, dance as madly as you like, and sing as loudly as you desire without putting your peace, love, and happiness on the line.

Love is always a local call. Love is reached through self-love. The fast track and hot route to love is self-love. Love yourself without attaching conditions to it.

And when you've done that, you've taken the first step. Then, a flowering will happen. You and your life will begin to blossom into something tremendously beautiful, something incredibly blissful.

You've heard it before, but it's true: "Be yourself and love yourself—everybody else is already taken!"

You're the leading edge of you!

No matter your faults, failures, or foibles, you're the best you—because you're the only you—there ever has been. That will always be true, even on your worst day.

SELF-ACCEPTANCE
OVER SELF-IMPROVEMENT

People have it backward:

Self-improvement doesn't lead to self-acceptance—
self-acceptance leads to self-improvement!

In other words, by improving yourself, you will never accept yourself,
despite what you think, because you will always take that "I can be
better, I should be better" mindset with you into the future.

However, by accepting yourself now, you will become an improved, more
peaceful, more joyful, more loving version of yourself in no time.

The key to self-improvement is self-acceptance.

The more deeply you accept yourself, the more quickly, easily, and
effortlessly you begin to improve. The more deeply you accept your
"weaknesses," the more your weaknesses are transformed into strengths.

It's a miracle: That which you accept, disappears. That which you shine
the light of loving, nonjudgmental awareness on becomes light, too.

With loving, nonjudgmental awareness, all that is wrong will disappear from
your life. It won't happen overnight, but it will happen gradually, over time.

Stop trying so hard to always improve yourself. Accept
yourself, instead—then, life will improve you.

Relax and accept yourself—then, you will blossom. You will flower.
When you accept yourself, your natural gifts will start growing.

Accept yourself, and you will fulfill your potential, whatever it is.
Accept your ordinariness, and you will become extraordinary!

Jesus accepted himself—that is how he became Christ.

Siddhartha accepted himself—that is how he became Buddha.

Accept yourself, and you will be transformed into
something extraordinarily beautiful, too!

If you don't accept yourself, no amount of self-improvement can ever change that. No amount of self-improvement can ever make up for a lack of self-acceptance.

Unless you're happy with yourself, you won't be happy with anything in your life—with where you are, with what you do, with what you have, or with whom you spend your time.

I like what Robert Holden says. He says, "My teaching isn't a teaching in self-improvement intended to create a new you. My teaching is a teaching in self-acceptance designed to help you recover the *original* you."

DON'T COMPETE AND YOU CAN'T BE BEAT

Don't compete with other people, and don't compare
yourself to other people, either.

You are one of a kind. You're the best you there ever was.

Nobody in the world is inferior; nobody in the world is
superior; and nobody in the world is equal, either!

We are all unique, one-of-a-kind.

Remember this little expression. It's a mnemonic device:
"When you don't compete, you can't be beat!"

When you don't compete, there's no competition. When
you don't compare, you are incomparable!

Drop comparison, and everything is already perfect. You
are perfect, and life is perfect already, too.

LOVE ISN'T SACRIFICE

People have the wrong idea about love and sacrifice.

Almost everybody confuses love with sacrifice, but love is not sacrifice.

Almost everybody confuses sacrifice with love, but sacrifice is not love.

Love is joy, but sacrifice is fear. Love is joyful, but sacrifice is fearful. Love is joy-based, but sacrifice is fear-based.

Love is overflowing bliss, and sacrifice is overflowing fear.

Love never asks for sacrifice—only *fear* asks for sacrifice. Only insecurity asks for sacrifice.

Love is the *absence* of sacrifice, and sacrifice is the *absence* of love.

True love doesn't require sacrifice. If it requires sacrifice, it's not true love.

PRICE AND VALUE, LOVE AND SACRIFICE

People erroneously conflate sacrifice with love in the
same way they conflate price with value.

When you don't know the real value of something, you
look at its price to inform you of its value.

Likewise, when you don't know what real love is, you look at the
sacrifice made to inform you of whether or not it's real love.

The higher the price paid for an item, the more value people place on that
item. The more a thing costs, the more valuable they think that thing is.

Likewise, the greater the sacrifice made for a relationship, the more
value they assign to that relationship. The more a relationship
costs, the more valuable they think that relationship is.

In other words, people think of sacrifice as the price paid for
love, but love never comes with a price tag. Love is always freely
given and freely received... or else it is not love at all.

There are no strings attached to real love. There are no
expectations or demands. Love is not a business affair or
business negotiation. It is neither ambitious nor political.

Sacrifice keeps score, but love *never* keeps score.

People associate value with price, and they associate love with
sacrifice, but that's all really faulty, fuzzy, lazy logic.

JUST SAYIN'...

Are you waiting for the world to love and believe in
you before you love and believe in yourself?

The world didn't love and believe in Jesus—
before Jesus loved and believed in himself.

The world didn't love and believe in Buddha—
before Buddha loved and believed in himself.

Martin Luther King, Jr., Mandela, JFK, Gandhi, Oprah,
Michael Jordan, Obama... Whoever!

Come on. Give it up. It's hopeless.

Love and believe in yourself already!

LOVE IS LIFE-AFFIRMATIVE

Never think that self-denial, self-sacrifice, or self-betrayal is a good thing.

Self-betrayal is still betrayal; self-sacrifice is still
sacrifice; and self-denial is still denial.

In fact, self-betrayal is the highest betrayal; self-sacrifice is the
lowest sacrifice; and self-denial is the worst denial.

If you have betrayed yourself, who is left to help the world?

If you have sacrificed yourself, who is left to accept the world?

If you have denied yourself, who is left to love the world?

Real love is never life-denying—real love is always life-affirming.

If you look deeply into Jesus' teaching, Buddha's teaching, and Lao Tzu's teaching,
you will find this to be true. All of their teachings were life-affirmative.

Contrary to popular opinion, they weren't martyrs—they were merry-makers!

They weren't merry-makers in the way many people think of merry-making—
they sought lasting, inner fulfillment, not just fleeting, outer pleasure.

That's real merry-making in my book. That's real
peace, love, and joy in my experience.

How can giving up that which is *nothing* (empty and unfulfilling) for
that which is *everything* (fulfilling) be considered a sacrifice?

How can giving up that which you never wanted in the first place—
fear, separation, unhappiness—be considered a "sacrifice"?

That's not sacrifice—that's celebration!

When Jesus, Buddha, and Lao Tzu taught "self-denial" and "denying
yourself," they were teaching the denial of your misery-making self.

They were teaching denial of your false self—your ego, your
fearful self, your mind-made self, your body-attached self, your
pleasure-chasing self, your illusory sense of a separate self.

Jesus, Buddha, and spiritual teachers like them teach the denial of your
misery-making self, not the denial of your merry-making self!

They teach people to dive more deeply into life—real life, divine life,
the life within you (God)—to discover true peace, love, and joy.

They teach people to dive more deeply into themselves—their true selves, their divine selves—to discover the true source of peace, love, and joy.

Jesus and Buddha didn't renounce life—they renounced misery!

They didn't renounce life—they lived life, real life!

They weren't sacrificial lambs—they were true, celebratory leaders!

Buddha gave up his ascetic lifestyle to become enlightened. Jesus drank wine and spent more time at weddings, festivals, and feasts—teaching people the truth within their own Being—than anywhere else.

This isn't renunciation—this is revelry!

Don't escape life—embrace life! Embrace *real* life, divine life!

Don't deny yourself, sacrifice yourself, or betray yourself. Accept yourself, celebrate yourself, and commit to yourself.

Your true Self, your spiritual Self, your God-Self.

The Self.

CARPET YOUR OWN FEET

Once upon a time, there lived a king.

The king, tired of walking around the kingdom barefoot, created
a law. According to the law, the entire kingdom was to be
carpeted so that he could walk around more comfortably.

Of course, this kind of project was expensive. So, in order to pay
for this project, the king had to wage war on the entire world.

Hearing of the news, the court jester couldn't contain
his laughter. He ridiculed the king.

"How silly," he said. "The king is so stupid. He is creating
unnecessary work and trouble for us all. And for what? So he
can walk around more comfortably? Ha! What idiocy!"

The king, overhearing the court jester ridiculing him, was outraged.
He yelled, "What are you laughing at, you silly little man?"

The court jester, not wanting to insult the king but unable to contain
his amusement, responded: "If you are uncomfortable walking around
the kingdom in your bare feet, why not just carpet your own feet? Why
wage war on the whole world so that you can carpet your kingdom?
It's so much easier and cheaper to carpet your own feet!"

The king was dumbstruck. "What a simple answer from a simple
man," he thought. "Why hadn't I thought of that?"

We laugh at the king's silly proposition, but how many of us do the same
thing? How many of us wage war on the entire world in an attempt to
achieve peace, love, and happiness in our own hearts and souls?

How many of us ask the entire world—our partners, our kids,
our family, our friends, our colleagues, our enemies, everyone
really—to be different so that we can be happy?

Like the king in the story, we don't need to carpet the whole
world—we only need to carpet our own feet.

When we carpet our own feet, we are comfortable everywhere we go,
no matter where we go. We don't impose impossible standards and
unnecessary expectations on other people, the world, or life itself.

Instead of asking other people or the world to change,
all we really need to do is change ourselves.

All we really need to do is make ourselves more comfortable. When
we are more comfortable, the whole world is more comfortable.
When we are more peaceful, loving, and joyful, the whole world
is a more peaceful, loving, and joyful place to live.

I cannot say it enough: Never wait for anybody or anything to
change before you get happy. Nothing ever changes in your
life, at least not in a lasting way, until *you* change.

Then, everything changes all at once.

The biggest change in the world, the one that fuels all other changes, is self-change.

The best help is self-help; the best love is self-love.

SELF-LOVE IS NOT EGOTISTICAL

There's nothing in the world that can complete you, fulfill you, or fill you up. You are complete, fulfilled, and full already—you just don't know it.

Despite what people think, this does not mean being "full of ego." People who are "full of ego" or "full of themselves" do not feel full inside. They do not feel fulfilled.

Egotistical people often come across as conceited, but the truth is that they are anything but secure inside. Underneath their seemingly conceited exterior lies a dark, insecure interior. Underneath the outer display of arrogance lies insecurity and fear.

By appearance, the ego is a display of outward abundance and fullness. In reality, however, the ego is actually a feeling of overwhelming emptiness and deep, inner lack. The ego is a sense of "not enough-ness"—not doing enough, not having enough, and not being enough.

"I am not enough; I don't have enough; and I don't do enough"— that's ego. The ego is a poverty mindset, and "poverty" is always a statement about your inner reality, not your outer circumstances.

For instance, the ego says, "I want that thing or that person. I want that thing or person, because that thing or person will make me feel better about myself. That thing or person, especially if other people see me with that thing or person, will make me *more*. It will make me more special. It will make me more loved or likeable. Somehow, in some way, by being associated with that, whatever that is, I will be happier."

"Finally, I will be somebody!" That's ego. That desire is coming from a place of lack: the ego.

Of course, the truth is that you can't become somebody, because you *already* are somebody.

Not knowing that is "ego."

Knowing that is "self-love."

YOUR GIFT TO THE WORLD

Loving yourself is your gift to the world.

When you love yourself, you are saving the world
from a thousand and one problems.

When you don't love yourself, however, you create
all kinds of problems for the world.

Through your self-hate and misery, you create hell on earth;
but through your self-love and happiness, you help to create
heaven on earth. You help to create a new earth.

Heaven and hell aren't geographical places outside of you—
they are spiritual places *within* you. They are attitudes.

A devil isn't somebody who goes to hell someday, and an
angel isn't somebody who goes to heaven someday.

A devil is somebody who carries his hell with him wherever he goes, and an
angel is somebody who carries her heaven with her wherever she goes.

A devil is somebody who turns everywhere he goes into a hell, and an
angel is somebody who transforms everywhere she goes into a heaven.

Understanding this means never having to tell anybody who judges, criticizes,
insults, or attacks you to "go to hell" again, because you know they are there
already. In their self-hate and misery, they live in hell year-round; there is
nowhere else for them to go. Wherever they go, they carry their hell with them.

Believe it or not, when you love yourself and are truly happy, you are
taking care of all of us. You are loving all of us. You are an angel, and your
presence is creating heaven on earth, whether you know it or not.

Chapter 6

LONELINESS, ALONENESS & ALL-ONENESS

Love starts with self-love.

And self-love just means enjoying your own company.

It means learning to be happy without a partner,
so you can be happy with one, too.

ENJOYING YOUR ALONENESS

Aloneness isn't loneliness, and loneliness isn't aloneness.

You can be alone but not lonely, and you can be lonely but not alone.

You can be all by yourself and yet feel happy and deeply loved. On the other hand, you can be in a large crowd, surrounded by thousands of people, but feel sad, completely unloved, and all alone. Isn't this true?

I love what Jean Paul-Sartre says. He says, "If you are lonely when you're alone, you are in bad company."

Loneliness has nothing to do with who is around you and everything to do with what is *inside* you.

If you know how to enjoy your aloneness, you can always be happy. If you know how to love your own company, you can feel loved—and "be in love"—at all times.

If you don't know how to enjoy your aloneness, however, you will be miserable and lonely, even in a crowd. You will be miserable and lonely, even in a relationship with the most loving person in the world.

You will be miserable and lonely with even a Jesus or a Buddha as your partner!

The key, then, is to learn how to love your aloneness.

When you learn to love your aloneness, your loneliness disappears, and all that's left is love.

Erich Fromm agrees. He says, "The ability to be alone is the condition for the ability to love."

LET GO OF THE DROP

We live in an ocean of love.

We live, move, and have our being in love. In reality, there is nothing but love.

Love happens—is *felt*—when you let go of the drop and become the ocean.

It happens—is *felt*—when you let go of your illusion of separateness
and realize your oneness with life and all life forms.

When you drop your illusion of separateness, you don't just dissolve into the
ocean of love; you realize that you've always been dissolved into the ocean of love.

You are not the wave—you are the water!

You are not the drop—you are the ocean!

Let go of the drop and become the ocean already! Let go of the *thought* that
you are just a drop and realize that you have always been the ocean!

ALONENESS AND TOGETHERNESS

Meditation just means being joyful by yourself.

That's all meditation is: learning how to enjoy your aloneness.

Meditation is finding bliss in your aloneness, and love is sharing
the bliss you found in your aloneness with the world.

Meditation gives you bliss, and love lets you share it.

Meditation and love are both needed. Aloneness
and togetherness are both necessary.

You should be able to enjoy yourself—that is meditation. And
you should be able to enjoy others, too—that's love.

When you can enjoy yourself and enjoy others, too, you are healthy and whole.

You are "holy."

Until you are capable of finding blissfulness in your aloneness, you
will never be capable of finding blissfulness in your togetherness.

Meditation is the science of finding blissfulness in your aloneness,
and love is the art of sharing your blissfulness with the world.

THE PENDULUM OF LOVE

Love and joy should really be one word: "love-joy."

Or, perhaps it should be: "joy-love!" since joy should always come first.

In either case, love and joy are not two different energies—
they are two ways of seeing the *same* thing. They are not two
things—they are two perceptions of the *same* energy.

When you are alone or introverted, it is called "joy;" but when
you are with others or extroverted, it is called "love."

We should all be pendulums, swinging from one to the other—
from ingoing joy to outgoing joy, from ingoing love to outgoing
love, from aloneness to togetherness... and back again.

Aloneness energizes the battery, and togetherness exhausts the battery; aloneness
charges the battery, and togetherness drains the battery. Aloneness fills you
up, and togetherness empties you so that aloneness can fill you up again.

Love creates a great need and desire to be alone, and
aloneness creates a great need and desire to love.

Meditation and love are both needed, not just one or the other.

The whole woman—the "holy" woman—spends time alone, and she spends
time with others, too. The whole man is both meditative and loving.

Enjoy yourself and enjoy others, too. Enjoy your aloneness and enjoy
your togetherness, too. Enjoy your meditation and enjoy your love,
also! When you are bored with one, swing into the other.

Please don't get stuck in one extreme or the other.

If the swing gets stuck to one side, the entire pendulum—not just
one half of the pendulum—is broken. The pendulum only remains
a pendulum, a functioning mechanism, if there is no clinging,
no grasping, and no attachment to one side or the other.

In other words, love is impossible without joy, but joy is incomplete without love.

Aloneness and togetherness—joy and love—are two sides of the same coin.

Meditation gives you bliss, and love lets you share that bliss with others.

Meditation gives you God, and love lets you share that godliness with other people.

Meditation gives you divine abundance, and love lets you
share that divine abundance with the world!

Meditation makes you rich, but love makes you wealthy!

"BESIDE YOURSELF"

Remember this phrase: "beside yourself."

When you are "beside yourself," you are worried, upset, or otherwise unhappy. You feel like two people. You are divided inside. You are double-minded. You are conflicted inside. You are at war with yourself.

It's a miserable experience, but a beautiful expression: "beside yourself."

It's as if you and your evil twin are sitting next to each other, and you don't know who is who. You are beside—"by the side of"—yourself. You feel that you are no longer one. You feel like you're sort of split into two people.

When you are beside yourself, you are under the ultimate illusion: the illusion of separateness, the illusion that there is—or could ever be—two of you.

The truth is that there is only one of you.

In fact, there is only one of all of us.

There is only One, period.

Dive deep within yourself. If you dig deep enough
inside, you'll discover the real you.

And when you find it, you'll discover something else divine, too: The real you is the same as the real me... and the real everybody else, too.

ALONE OR "ALL-ONE"

Look closely at this word: "alone."

Think about the word "alone," but don't be fooled by it. On the surface, aloneness looks like separateness. Beneath the surface, however, aloneness isn't separateness at all.

Aloneness is connectedness; it is connectedness with the All.

When you are "alone," you are "all one." You are "all one" with yourself, "all one" with life, and "all one" with all life forms.

"All-one-ness" is divine!

Sometimes people say, "There is only one God," but I think they are missing a comma or, perhaps, a colon.

I think what they really mean is this: "There is only one: God." That's the way I see it.

Really, you could drop the word "God" and just stick with the simple statement, "There is only One." That sums it up just perfectly.

Always remember that when you are alone, you are all one with everything and everybody.

If you think differently, stop thinking and the problem is instantly solved.

In fact, stop thinking, and *all* problems are instantly solved.

No thinking, no problem.

WHAT RELATIONSHIP?

Here's a consolation for all of you who might be worried about
not being in—or having—a romantic relationship...

From the highest perspective, relationships don't exist.

From the highest perspective, a relationship requires two separate selves,
but there is no such thing as a separate self. No selves are ever separate.

Separateness does not exist—only oneness exists. We are all just one.

The only thing ever happening is oneness.

Bodies appear separate and minds seem separate, but
we are neither our bodies nor our minds.

At the deepest level, at the level of reality, we are simply life itself.

We are awareness itself. We are presence itself. We are consciousness itself.

If all of us are the One Life that underlies all life forms, what
is left for any of us to have a relationship with?

Forms relate, but the formless simply is.

From the highest perspective, not only is a relationship with
others impossible, but—and this should seem somewhat obvious
now—even a relationship with yourself is impossible.

From the highest perspective, you can't really love yourself, and you can't really
hate yourself, either. You can't accept yourself, and you can't reject yourself, either.

All you can do is *be* yourself.

When you are just being yourself—just being, period—you are one. You are one
with yourself, one with life, and one with everybody and everything in life.

The only thing that can ever block that awareness is a thought.

If you're not convinced, just try it: Enter into stillness and silence. Don't let
even one thought interrupt that sacred serenity, and see if this isn't true.

Without thinking about anything at all, see if you
experience anything like separateness at all.

RELATING, NOT RELATIONSHIP

As long as you have the idea of a "relationship" in your mind, you will suffer.

As long as you are concerned about having or not
having a relationship, you will suffer.

As long as you think, "I have a relationship" or "I
don't have a relationship," you will suffer.

As long as you think, "I am in a relationship" or "I am not in a
relationship," regardless of with whom, you will suffer.

The concept of "relationship" is loaded with expectations,
and that's why you will always suffer.

That concept is loaded with expectations of what a "relationship"
should be—what it should look like and feel like.

When you try to make *reality* conform to these *unreal* concepts, you will
always suffer, because life doesn't follow your logic. Life has its own
logic, and that logic has nothing to do with your ideas about it.

The truth is simply this: There are no relationships.
Relationships, as such, don't exist.

There are no relationships—there is only the present moment.

And in the present moment, there are no relationships—there is only *relating*.

How we relate—how well we love—depends on how empty we are
of ideas, not only about relationships but about everything!

The emptier you are of ideas about love, the fuller your
experience of love will be; the fewer expectations you have
about love, the greater your experience of love will be!

The fewer the expectations, the greater your enjoyment.

TRANSFORMING LONELINESS
INTO LOVINGNESS

When you're lonely, you're missing somebody, but that
somebody is not somebody else—that somebody is *you!*

When *you* are lonely, *you* are the one missing in your life, not anybody else.
Somebody else isn't absent from your life—*you're* absent from your life.

When you know the secret, when you've learned how to love your aloneness,
there is nothing better, more beautiful, or more blissful than being alone.

A happy person is so happy that she wants to be left alone to be happy.

You cannot make a woman who loves her aloneness and enjoys
her solitude unhappy, because she has learned how to be joyful
under all conditions. She has learned to be joy itself. Even in her
aloneness—especially in her aloneness—she is happy.

Alone, she is self-sufficient. Alone, she is a light unto herself.

Through aloneness you get to know yourself. When you get
to know yourself, you get to know the meaning of life. You get
to experience the significance and splendor of life.

Aloneness is your temple. It is God's temple. It is the place within you
where Source lives. When you have stood alone in your own being, in Being
itself—in your light, in your love—you have found your real home.

You are an empress, and the whole world is your empire.

You are a king, and the entire universe is your kingdom.

You don't need to conquer the world, because you have already conquered it!

You don't have to conquer anybody else, because you've already conquered
yourself, and that is the only real, meaningful conquest in the world!

Until you learn how to conquer your own kingdom, don't go out
into the world looking for other kingdoms to conquer.

Until you know how to be blissful even in your aloneness, forget
all about love for now—just work on being blissful, instead.

Until you can transform your loneliness into
lovingness, you are not yet ready for love.

Before you go deeply into a relationship with another, go deeply into a relationship with yourself. Before you go deeply into a relationship, go deeply into yourself.

Before you go deeply into a relationship, go deeply into meditation—that's what I'm saying.

If you don't go deeply into meditation—if you don't learn the art of loving your aloneness—before you go deeply into a relationship, your problems won't just be added to.

They will be multiplied.

KNOW YOURSELF TO LOVE YOURSELF

I'd like to clarify something here about loving yourself.

This point is often missed by most people, but it's a significant contribution to the conversation on self-love, in the way that I mean it.

If you want to love yourself, you have to get to know yourself—your true Self, your spiritual Self—first.

Loving yourself is impossible unless you know yourself.

You don't know yourself yet—how can you love yourself? If you don't know yourself, what will you even love?

In other words, to love yourself, don't start by loving yourself.

No, if you start by loving yourself, you'll only love your false self, not your true Self.

You'll only love the unreal, not the real. You'll only love the trivial, the insignificant, the nonessential, the things that *aren't* you—your real Self—at all.

You'll only love forms, not the formless.

You'll only love your possessions, your power, your prestige, and your position. You'll love your body, your mind, and your personality—your ego, your false self.

None of these things are the real you.

What's more, none of these things are even *yours*. They don't belong to you. You think they belong to you, but they don't. They are all on loan to you.

On the deepest level, of course, even that isn't true. On the deepest level, these things don't exist in the way you think they do. They are all mind-made illusions that disappear over the course of time.

They are ephemeral—not eternal. They are finite— not infinite. Hence, they are not "real."

Only this which is infinite and eternal is what we call "real."

To love yourself, then, don't start by loving yourself. Instead, start by *knowing* yourself. When you know yourself, you'll automatically start loving yourself.

And to know yourself, start with meditation.

The more you meditate, the more you'll come to know yourself. And the more you come to know yourself, the more you'll come to love yourself.

Meditation is priority number one.

Meditation is always primary; love is secondary.

The more you meditate, the more you'll get to know yourself—your true Self, your spiritual Self.

Then, love, including what I call "self-love," will happen on its own. You won't have to do anything to make it happen.

It will happen all by itself.

KNOWING YOURSELF IS LOVING YOURSELF

Let's go deeper.

Knowing yourself doesn't really *lead* to loving yourself.

Knowing yourself *is* loving yourself.

To know yourself *is* to love yourself, too.

Knowing yourself and loving yourself are not two different things—they are two ways of seeing the same thing. They are two ways of talking about the same phenomenon.

To know yourself *is* to love yourself, and to love yourself *is* to know yourself—they are two sides of the same coin.

And the name of that coin is "meditation."

When you meditate, you know yourself and love yourself all in one fell swoop. It is not three steps—meditate, know yourself, and love yourself.

It's only one step: meditate.

In other words, meditation doesn't *lead* to knowing yourself, and knowing yourself doesn't *lead* to loving yourself.

Meditation *is* knowing yourself, and meditation *is* loving yourself, too. Meditation is self-knowledge, and meditation is self-love, too.

MEDITATION IS BEING YOURSELF, KNOWING YOURSELF, AND LOVING YOURSELF

Meditation is loving nothing, knowing nothing, and being nothing.

In other words, the more you meditate, the more you understand that there is nothing to know, nothing to love, and nothing to be.

Meditation is realizing that:

I am nothing—"no-thing."

I am nobody—"no-body."

Meditating, being yourself, knowing yourself, and loving yourself all mean the same thing: silence, stillness, and spaciousness.

In that silence, stillness, and spaciousness—in that serenity—there is nothing to be, and nobody to be it; there is nothing to know, and nobody to know it; and there is nothing to love, and nobody to love it.

There is only awareness, consciousness, or presence.

There is only life and felt oneness with life.

There is only love.

MEDITATION IS WHAT YOU ARE

In the end, meditation isn't something you *do*.

It's something you *are*.

You *are* meditation.

In the end, being yourself, knowing yourself, and
loving yourself isn't something you *do*.

It's something you *are*.

You are existence (being), consciousness (knowing), and bliss (loving).

That's the deepest understanding possible, and it's not an understanding at all.

It's the greatest experience possible, and it's not an experience at all.

It just is.

•

POOR IN SPIRIT, RICH IN LOVE

Jesus says, "Blessed are the poor in spirit: for theirs is the kingdom of heaven."

When you become poor in spirit, you don't enter heaven—heaven enters you!

In fact, when you become poor in spirit—egoless, empty, and
aware of your intrinsic oneness—you realize that heaven can't
enter you, because heaven never left you in the first place.

Heaven—the presence of love, the presence of life—
always has been and always will be within you.

Jesus says, "They can't say, 'Here it is!' or 'There it is!'
You see, the kingdom of God is within you."

The presence of life (God) is within you.

Love is just knowing that, realizing that, feeling that.

Being that.

IN-JOY-IN-YOURSELF

Meditation—practicing the Presence—puts you in touch with your joy.

Joy just means enjoying your aloneness. Joy just means loving your aloneness.

Spend some time each day getting acquainted with yourself.

Most people remain strangers to themselves for their entire lifetime.
For the rest of your life, you will have to spend every second with
yourself, so you might as well get familiar with yourself.

If given the chance, most people would divorce themselves.

Unfortunately, you are the only person you can't get rid of. You are the only person
in the world you can't divorce. For all of eternity, you are going to be with yourself.

Can you live with this person forever? Can you live
happily-ever-after with this person?

Until you learn to live happily with yourself—until you learn how
to transform your loneliness into love, until you learn how to
love your aloneness—you are not yet ready for real love.

In other words, the litmus test for love is unconditional joy.

Are you ready for love? Can you be joyful in all
circumstances and under all conditions?

In other words, when you are totally alone, can you
still feel happy? Can you still feel love?

If you can say "yes," you have attained. If you cannot say "yes," please stay
home—figuratively, not literally—and learn to love your aloneness.

The mark of a happy woman is one who, when left alone with nothing
but her own thoughts to keep her company, is happy, nonetheless.

Love is a very simple phenomenon when you understand it: In order for
other people to enjoy your company, *you* must enjoy your company.

The art of love is joy, and the art of joy is meditation—loving your aloneness.

Meditation is a knack—the knack of relating to yourself
with love, kindness, and compassion.

Once you learn how to relate to yourself in that way—with loving-kindness—
you can relate to anybody and everybody in the world in that way, too.

EMPTINESS EMBRACED, FULLNESS FOUND

There are two types of people in the world:

People who don't accept their inner emptiness and try to stuff it with things; and people who accept their inner emptiness and don't try to stuff it with anything.

There are people who try to *escape* their inner emptiness
and people who *embrace* their inner emptiness.

The art of love is meditation, and meditation is just looking into—
and embracing—your inner emptiness. It is just welcoming your inner
emptiness—enjoying it and embracing it—with no desire to fill it.

There is no need to fill it, because it is full already—it just looks
empty. It is overflowing with everything you really want already!

Now listen to this closely, because this will take deep insight and a penetrating
eye to see: The closer you get to a truth, the more it appears to be a paradox.
The more something looks like a paradox, the closer you often are to a truth.

The concepts of emptiness and fullness look like
contradictions, but they are, in fact, complements.

Emptiness and fullness are not opposites—they are complements.

Emptiness embraced is fullness found.

That's the truth—not a contradiction, but a spiritual truth.

If you're looking for love, please don't try to fill your inner
emptiness with a thousand and one things.

Instead, look into it. Welcome it. Enjoy it. Embrace it. Become one with it.

When you look deeply into your inner emptiness, you'll see it transform itself
before your very eyes. That inner emptiness will become divine fullness!

When you are not, love is.

When you are empty, love fills you up.

More accurately, when you are empty, you discover that you
are full—and have *always* been full—of love already.

What Bruce Lee says is right: "The usefulness of a cup is its emptiness."

CREATING SPACE FOR LOVE

When you create a well, you are really just creating space.

You are creating space for the water—which is hidden
but can't be expressed—to express itself.

Likewise, when you are egoless, you are creating space.

You are creating space for the love—which is hidden
but can't be expressed—to express itself.

When you become egoless—empty inside without trying to stuff it with anything
or anybody from the outside—you don't have to go out and find love.

You just stay where you are, and love finds you.

In fact, you just stay where you are, and you realize love is *what* you are.
It is what you have always been, and it is what you will always be.

You realize that you *are* nothing but love.

In other words, love is already the case—just get out of the way already!

Just learn to be still and silent inside.

The rest will happen on its own.

•

BE LAST TO BE FIRST

Jesus says, "Those who are last will be first, and those who are first will be last."

When you are not concerned with being first—because you know you
already are somebody—you are closest to realizing true love.

In other words, when you are egoless—empty of loveless, lonely,
unhappy thoughts of separation—you don't find love someday.

You have found love today, already.

Chapter 7

YOUR PRESENCE, LOVE'S PRESENCE

Love is presence, and presence is love.

THE AGE OF DISTRACTION

To love anybody, you have to be present when you're with them.

The more present you are, the more available to love you are.

The art of true love is presence. Presence means paying attention to whoever and whatever is in your life right now, without letting your thoughts get in the way.

To love somebody, you have to remain undistracted. If you are distracted by other concerns, worries, and thoughts in your mind, you cannot love.

Love means paying attention to the present moment—and whomever or whatever it contains—without judgment.

More accurately, love means paying attention to Presence itself—the presence of life or God within yourself and everybody else—without judgment.

When you are present, when you are practicing the presence of life or God within yourself and everybody else—instead of judging anything or anybody—you are loving everybody and everything already.

You *are* love already.

•

PRACTICING THE PRESENCE OF LOVE

Love means giving the now all of your attention.

It means giving the eternal now—the only place where love exists—all of your loving attention.

When you give the present—Presence itself—all of your attention, you are practicing the presence of love.

In other words, *being love* means *being present*. It means being Presence itself.

When you are present—when you are Presence itself, when you are aware of your oneness with life and all life forms—love flows into, through, and out of you into everything and everybody around you.

When you are present—Presence itself—you allow the divine plan, which is always love, to express itself in, through, and *as* you and your life.

SLEEPWALKING THROUGH LIFE

A friend of mine has a grandmother.

Let's call her "Granny." Granny is five feet, three inches,
ninety years old, and grumpy as hell.

Granny lives by the clock. And when I say she "lives by the clock," I really mean it.

Sleepy or not, she goes to bed at precisely 8 P.M. Rested or not, she
wakes up at precisely 5 A.M. Hungry or not, she eats breakfast at
precisely 5:15 A.M., lunch at exactly 12 P.M., and dinner at 6 P.M. on
the nose. She never wavers from her schedule, no matter what.

This man, with whom Granny lives, has a grandfather clock in his home.
Unfortunately for Granny, this grandfather clock doesn't differentiate between
evening hours and morning hours, between A.M. and P.M. It could be 5 A.M. or
5 P.M., and you wouldn't be able to tell the difference based on the clock alone.

Granny does not—*will not*—consider any other factor in her daily
schedule except for this clock's time. She will not consider whether
it is daytime or nighttime, morning or evening, sunlit or moonlit. She
will not consider her own moods, and she will not take into account
her own body's needs; she won't consider her sleepiness or her own
satiety signals. Granny lives her life by the clock, pure and simple.

Well, I cannot tell you the number of times Granny has gone to
bed at 8 A.M., gotten up at 5 P.M., eaten breakfast at 5:15 P.M.,
eaten lunch at midnight, and eaten dinner at 6 A.M.

Usually, when somebody is there to correct her, Granny doesn't do all of that on
the same day. Usually, part of the way through the day, somebody notices that she's
off-schedule and corrects her, to her amazement, surprise, and dismay, of course.

Nonetheless, Granny lives by this schedule. If she is in the middle of dinner but
the clock chime goes off signaling that it's 8 P.M., she abruptly finishes her meal (or
not) and heads straight to bed. Never mind that she's wide-awake and still hungry.

If she hasn't slept a wink all night and the chime goes off signaling that
it's 5 A.M., she wakes up and prepares breakfast. Never mind that she,
then, falls asleep at the dining room table. The clock is the clock!

Granny never lives in the now, and because she never lives in the now, she is
sleepy all day, every day. Despite the fact that she can sleep whenever she wants to
sleep and as much as she wants to sleep, she is always tired. She, quite literally,

sleepwalks her way through life. She's always on auto-pilot. She's never awake enough to fully participate in anything. Bless her heart, she's never really, truly alive.

The other interesting thing about Granny is that, while she has access to food in abundance, she's always hungry. Still, she sticks to the clock. No matter how hungry or sleepy she is, she won't eat a snack or take a nap until the clock says it's time to do so. Now, to me, that just doesn't make any sense.

If poor Granny hasn't made her life difficult enough, she also complains about everything. In particular, she complains about how unloving everybody is toward her. Now, remember, the man she lives with purchased this very large, expensive house, and he invited his grandmother to live with him in it. Plus, he gave Granny the largest room in the house, even bigger than his own room. Finally, this man's chef cooks and prepares almost every meal for all of them—breakfast, lunch, and dinner.

Again, this doesn't make much sense to me. Clearly, Granny's life is full of love and happiness, but Granny doesn't feel it. Granny doesn't see it. Granny is not aware of it. She doesn't find any love or happiness in it.

It's sad, but true: Granny is one of those hungry ghosts that we spoke about earlier. She's hungry for love and happiness, but incapable of receiving it.

This all reminds me of that quote by Auntie Mame: "Life is a buffet and most damn folks are starving to death!"

We laugh at this story because Granny is starving—starving for food, starving for sleep, starving for love, and starving for happiness—in the midst of plenty. But how many of us are doing exactly the same thing in our lives?

How many of us are running our entire lives by some external clock, calendar, or schedule instead of living in the now?

How many of us are sleepwalking through our lives?

How many of us are starving—starving for peace, starving for love, or starving for joy—in the midst of plenty?

How many of us are really aware of the "pre-sent" peace, love, and joy that already exist inside ourselves?

How many of us are ever truly present in our lives?
How many of us are living in the moment?

In other words, you might be alive, but are you really living?

LACKING AN AWARENESS OF LOVE

There is only one problem in the world, and it's not
a lack of love, despite what I said earlier.

The only problem in the world is not a lack of love—the only
problem in the world is a lack of *awareness* of love.

There's enough love in us—we have access to infinite love—
but there's not enough *awareness* of that love.

There's enough love in us to solve any problem in the world, but there is not yet
enough awareness of that love to do so. The love within us is infinite, but we have
little-to-no awareness of it, so we have yet to really manifest that love in the world.

The reason that you might not feel, experience, and enjoy more love in
your life is not because there aren't enough loving people in the world—
other people have nothing to do with your experience of love.

The reason that you don't feel, experience, and enjoy more
love in your life is because your mind is full of too many
loveless thoughts—there is simply no room for love.

The love you are looking for is always right here, no matter where "here" is.

To know that's true, however, you have to be where love is: right
here. You have to be present. You have to be here, really here.

You can't be somewhere else, mentally living in some past moment, which
is already gone, or some future moment, which hasn't yet arrived.

Buddha says, "As you walk and eat and travel, be where you
are. Otherwise you will miss most of your life."

To enjoy life and find love, you have to be right here—aware of the
life and love inside you, aware of the life and love that *is* you.

Vince Vaughan, the actor, once said, "Where my body is, let my mind be, too."

That's right. That's presence. That's love, the art of love.

To discover the treasure that is hidden within this moment, you have to dive deeply
into this moment—not the last moment and not the next moment, but *this* moment.

Remember, love is always present—"pre-sent."

To feel, experience, and enjoy love, you have to be here
where love is. You have to be present.

To allow the divine to penetrate you—to let the divine express itself through you—you have to be available.

More accurately, to know the divine within you—to know the divine *is* you—you have to be aware of it, conscious of it.

That's what meditation is; that's what prayer is; that's what presence is; and that's what love, too, is: just being available to the love that's inside you, that *is* you, right here and now.

To the mystic, there is only one thing ever happening in the world, and that one thing is love—felt oneness with life (God).

Love is just life (God), *realized.*

Love is just life (God), *felt.*

YOUR PRESENCE IS LOVE'S PRESENCE

When you are present, love is present.

Or, more accurately, when you are present, you are
finally *aware* of love's *omnipresence.*

Love is always present, but you are not always aware of this
fact. When you are present, you finally experience love's
presence, which is always there, wherever "there" is.

Love is feeling the presence of the one life that underlies all forms. Love is
feeling the presence of that one life that is present in yourself and all others.

Love is simple. It means being aware of the divine within you and all others—
no matter where you are, what you're doing, or with whom you're doing it.

Love is ever-present.

The reason you don't feel, experience, and enjoy more love in your life is not
because love is not present. The reason you don't feel, experience, and enjoy more
love in your life is because *you* are not present to feel, experience, and enjoy it.

Love is present, but you are absent. You are distracted. You
are unaware of love's presence—and as—in your life.

To experience love you have to be where life is: the present. If you are mentally
living in some other moment, past or future, you will never find true love.

If you are full of too much past, too much future, and not enough
present—not enough Presence—there is not enough love in the
world to compensate for your lack of presence or awareness.

Manna could be raining down on your head from heaven, but you
wouldn't recognize it; you wouldn't be able to receive it.

WELCOME HOME

It's been said, "Home is where the heart is."

Indeed, home is where *love* is.

Since love is inside you at all times, home is anywhere
and everywhere in the world *you* are.

Wherever you go, you carry your home with you. Be present—aware
of this simple truth—and you're home, no matter where you are!

As long as you're present—conscious and aware of the presence of life
and love within you—you can never be anywhere other than home.

You can never be anything but comfortable, relaxed, and at peace.
You can never feel lonely or unloved, no matter where you go
and no matter who goes—or doesn't go—with you.

When you are present—when you are practicing the Presence—
you are always home, no matter where you are.

When you are present—when you are Presence itself—you
are always in heaven, no matter what is happening around you
and no matter what seems to be happening *to* you.

God, the presence of God, lives in you.

Since heaven is where God lives, you can't ever escape heaven.
You just have to be present, aware, or conscious of this fact.

Be present, and you're in heaven! Be present, and you're in paradise!

Presence is paradise. Presence—your presence, God's
presence—*is* heaven. It is your true home.

Living in the present—living *as* Presence—is heaven;
living in the past and future is hell.

To be present is to be in love; to be Presence itself is to *be* love.

To be absent—distracted, lost in thought, lost in
the past or future—is to not be in love.

It is to live in fear, loneliness, and separation.

LOVE IS NOT THINKING

You are not the mind.

You are the *awareness* behind the mind, the *awareness* beyond the mind.

You are Awareness itself.

There's something within you that remains unchanging—that's you, the real you.

To *know* it is "peace." To *be* it is "bliss." To *share* it is "love."

In other words, love is the experience and enjoyment of
life, not the evaluation and examination of it.

Love means *being* blissful—not just *thinking* about being blissful.

Love is a *being* thing—not a thinking thing. Love is *being*—not thinking.

Thoughts don't lead to love. Only *not* thinking—only
thoughtless, wordless awareness—leads to (and *is*) love.

If you are thinking about love, you aren't experiencing and
enjoying it. And if you are experiencing and enjoying it, you
aren't obsessively and compulsively thinking about it.

Love is Being, just being.

MINDFUL OR MIND FULL?

"Mindful" is an unfortunate term, because it appears to be something that it is not.

To be "mindful" does not mean to be "full of mind" or "full of thoughts." To be "mindful" means to be empty of thoughts but full of nonjudgmental awareness.

Being mindful is being aware of the fact that you're thinking thoughts about reality, not the truth about reality. Your thoughts, opinions, and judgments are just one way of thinking about things. You don't have to let them get in the way of peace, love, and happiness now.

All things, including thoughts and emotions, come and go. You don't have to take any of them seriously. You don't have to let them run and ruin your love life. You don't have to let them get in the way of feeling love now.

If you can learn to let all of these things pass through your awareness without judgment, condemnation, or criticism, you're left with only one thing: nonjudgmental awareness.

That nonjudgmental awareness *is* love.

With nonjudgmental awareness, you learn to stop believing everything you think. When you don't believe everything you think, you experience peace, love, and happiness right here and now.

In other words, stop thinking so much.

Then, you will find peace, love, and happiness right here.

Nothing else is needed.

FULL OF THOUGHTS OR FULL OF LOVE?

Let me repeat:

Contrary to what people think, to be "mindful" does not mean to be "full of mind."

It means to be "full of love!"

Love is just one thing: not letting your mind wander and roam all over the place.

Give whatever you're doing—breathing, walking, driving, listening to music, pouring tea, making love, whatever—your full attention.

Forget about the future and things you have to do; forget about the past and things you used to do; and focus on the present—on Presence itself—and things you *get* to do.

Mindfulness is a simple recognition: "I'm thinking thoughts— not reality. I'm thinking thoughts *about* reality, not reality itself. I'm living in my head—not real life."

Your thoughts are just one way of seeing things. There are other ways to see things, and none of those ways is 100 percent true, either, because they are still thoughts—not reality, which is always a thoughtless, wordless *experience*.

The more of these experiences you have—without condemnation, without judgment, with simple, loving awareness—the emptier your mind will become; the more gaps in thinking you will experience.

Those gaps are mini-satoris, mini-enlightenments.

Those gaps are moments of meditation, moments of love.

In those cracks, the light shines in. In those crevices, love enters you. In those spaces, love penetrates you.

In reality, of course, love doesn't enter or penetrate you at all— that's just a way of speaking. What really happens is that you simply come to realize what's always been the case:

You *are* love.

You realize that love is all there ever was, is, or could be. You realize that love has been there inside you—and everybody else—all along.

Enlightenment is the recognition that only love is real.

HUMAN LOVE TAKES TIME

Divine love takes no time, but human love sometimes takes time.

It doesn't have to take time, but it might, so please don't expect immediate results.

A Course in Miracles says, "Infinite patience produces immediate results."

The less patient you are, the slower it will happen. The more
patient you are, the faster it will happen. And when you
are infinitely patient, it will happen immediately.

The faster you go, the slower you arrive. The slower you go, the faster you arrive.
And when you don't go at all, you sometimes realize you are there already.

In other words, be patient, infinitely patient. Don't rush.

Don't rush life and don't rush love.

It takes nine months to make a baby. Source is all-powerful.
Surely, if it wanted, it could make a baby in much less time than
that. But it doesn't. It takes its time. It savors the process.

If you want to be like God, take your time! Be patient and savor it all.

Remember: Jesus never rushed, Buddha never rushed, and Lao Tzu never rushed.

Lao Tzu says, "Nature does not hurry, yet everything is accomplished."

Be like Jesus, be like Buddha, be like Lao Tzu, be like nature—don't rush!

Learn to touch life deeply with each breath and with
every step—love will track you down.

Learn to live in the here and now—everything else will take care of itself.

Learn to live in the moment—love will find you.

Learn to live in the present, learn to live as Presence itself. Then, you
will be love. You will become aware that you are love *already*.

STOP RUNNING AND REST

Unhappiness comes in two flavors: not getting what
you want and getting what you want.

When you don't get what you want, you suffer, because you didn't get
something you wanted. But when you get what you want, you suffer, too,
because, after you get it, you start worrying about losing it one day.

Most people worry themselves to death. Most people spend half of their lives
worrying about how to get and hold on to what they want... and the other half
worrying about how to get rid of and keep away what they don't want.

Most of us spend our entire lives running a rat race of one kind or another.
We spend our whole lives chasing all sorts of things—money, power, fame,
beauty, youth, health, happiness, love, relationships, children, whatever.

In other words, we spend our entire lives chasing happiness in one form or another.

No wonder we are so tired all the time! Our minds and bodies run all
day, every day, without taking even a single break or little rest. Even
in our sleep, our minds go on toiling and spinning, hurrying and
worrying, rushing and fussing, struggling, stressing, and straining.

The vast majority of us spend our entire lifetimes ruled by the ego: fear and desire.
We spend our whole lives ruled by thoughts, feelings, and actions of perceived lack.

We don't have to live this way—that's important to recognize.

We can stop running—physically and mentally. We can rest.

When we stop running and rest, a miracle happens: Everything we've been
looking for *finds us*. Everything we've been chasing starts *chasing us*.

Security and safety—it's right here!

Success, abundance, and true prosperity—it's all available right now!

Peace, love, and happiness—it's all here already!

When you stop and look, you find.

This is an entirely different approach. With this approach—by stopping
and looking deeply—you are not trying to get or hold on to anything,
and you are not trying to get rid or let go of anything, either.

Instead, you are simply stopping and looking. You are simply observing and looking deeply into it all without any judgment.

Without all the grasping, craving, and attachment
that spoil life, life becomes really alive.

When you learn to enjoy the infinite riches that are available to you—and *within* you—now, you find everything you've been looking for all along.

Lao Tzu is right, "By letting go, it all gets done."

By letting go, you discover that what you really want, you have already.

BE GOALLESS, BE AIMLESS

Sometimes I encourage people who are looking for love to be "goalless" or "aimless."

To be "goalless" or "aimless" means to do everything for the joy it brings,
not just for the successful outcome you're hoping to achieve through it.

It means to enjoy the journey as much as the destination. It
means to enjoy the process as much as the outcome.

Learn to do more things for enjoyment, and not only to
achieve some goal in a future that never arrives.

Whether it is meeting people, talking to people, flirting with people, dating
people, or whatever, do it for enjoyment. Do it because it's fun; have fun with it.

Whatever "it" is, if you can't enjoy it—if it's not fun and
you can't *make* it fun—try not to do it at all.

Don't do anything just to accomplish some goal or aim through it. Don't turn
anything—or *anybody*—into a means to some other end. That rarely turns out well.

Instead, learn to spread the end—peace, love, and joy—all over the means!

What this means is that you don't need an agenda to find love, because love
itself—feeling loved now, being loving now, and being happy now—*is* the agenda!

If you do that, the agenda will take care of itself.

Learn to cherish the present moment—learn to enjoy your
own presence, Presence itself—instead of putting goals in
front of you and running after them your whole life.

This is as true for finding love as it is for achieving success,
making money, or any other goal you have for yourself.

If you can be happy now, in time, you will find love and
everything else you want in your life, too.

When you are happy and truly fulfilled, you find yourself deeply loved already. You find your life overflowing with love already!

When you are truly happy, your greatest goal and highest purpose in life has already been achieved.

You have fulfilled your inner purpose (happiness) even while you are pursuing your outer purpose, even while you work toward your other, external goals.

LOVE IS INFINITELY PATIENT

You don't know where you came from, and you don't know where you are going.

You don't know where you were before you were born, and
you don't know where you are going after you die.

You may think you know based on your religious or spiritual beliefs, but
you don't really know based on your actual, personal experience.

That's called "no coming, no going."

You hurry and worry your whole life away only to reach nowhere—
now here. If you don't know where you are coming from or where you
are going to, why the hurry and worry? Why the rush and fuss?

That's why the entire practice is to stop running. Stop chasing the next moment,
the next experience, the next person, the next relationship, the next everything.

The more patient you are, the more quickly love—and everything
else you really want—will manifest in your life.

The more hurried you are, the more slowly love—and everything else
you really want—will manifest in your life, *if* it manifests at all.

The faster you go, the slower it happens; the slower you go, the faster it happens.
And when you don't (feel the need to) go at all, it seems to happen right away.

That's enlightenment!

Knowing that—*living* that—is enlightenment.

Remember, "Infinite patience produces immediate results."

That's true, because finding true love—and anything
else you want—is not a question of time.

It's a question of *mind*—the quality of your mind.

It really is true: "Love is patient." In fact, love is infinitely patient.

Love is infinitely patient, because love knows there is nowhere to go that offers a greater opportunity for fulfillment than the present moment, than this red-hot moment right here!

In fact, it's only the present moment that offers *any* opportunity for fulfillment at all.

STOP, DROP, AND ROLL

The next time you feel that anything is missing in your
life, no matter what it is, become present.

Presence makes you aware of the precious, prosperous
present moment where nothing is *ever* missing.

Remember: "If something is missing in my life, it must be *me*."

"No matter what I think is missing from my life right now, it's really
just me. I'm not present. I'm missing this precious, prosperous present
moment, and that's why I feel poor, sad, lonely, or unloved."

Then, let there be a pause; let there be a moment of silence.

With presence, you find everything you're looking for, and you find it immediately.

With your presence—which is always, simultaneously, the
presence of everything you really want or need—you find
everything you are looking for, and you find it immediately.

The next time you feel unhappy, take a tip from small children
and remember this simple mantra: "Stop, drop, and roll."

"Stop" what you're doing.

"Drop" what you're thinking.

And "roll" with the moment!

When you stop, drop, and roll, you escape the fiery furnace of
the ego—your thoughts and feelings of lack, loneliness, and
lovelessness—and you find true peace, love, and joy.

And you find it all without moving a single finger!

LOVE THIS MOMENT

Living a life of love means appreciating every moment you have.

It means never reducing any moment into a means to some other end.

It means valuing every moment—in its own right and for its own sake—because every moment, no matter what it contains, is yet another opportunity (and in fact, the *only* opportunity) to experience true love: to love yourself and others.

Despite—or, rather, *because* of—what they think, most people are in too much of a hurry to love. They are too busy to love.

People always think that, once they find a partner, they'll slow down and enjoy life. But that's simply not true.

You take yourself with you wherever you go, so you will take that same hurrying and worrying mindset, that same rushing and fussing attitude, with you into the future.

No matter what you think, you will not suddenly—one day, once you've found a partner—stop, slow down, and smell the roses.

If you want tomorrow to be different, you have to make *today* different. If you want tomorrow to be different, you have to start today. There is no other way.

Be today who you want to be tomorrow—that is the only way!

A PRACTICE FOR LOVERS

If you want to learn the art of love, here's a good practice to start...

Take any routine activity that is usually a means to some other end—activities like cleaning the floor, washing the dishes, folding the laundry, walking the dog, driving to work, and so on—and make it an end itself.

Don't reduce anything—or *anybody*—into a means to some other end. Focus on the action itself, not the fruit of your action. Focus on the person, not what you can get from that person.

If you are planted in the present and rooted in this moment, the fruit will take care of itself.

Give your full attention to the doing itself, and your doing will not only be much more effective; it will be much more fulfilling, too.

Turn every moment, activity, interaction, and relationship into an end itself. Don't sacrifice any moment, activity, interaction, or relationship for any other one.

As Eckhart Tolle says, "The present moment and whatever it contains is your friend, not your enemy and not an obstacle to be overcome."

Don't do anything just to get it over with!

Give whatever—and whoever—is in front of you right now all of your loving attention. If you do, the feeling that the activity is a nuisance—or that the person is a burden—will go away.

The result: Love will blossom inside you again! Then, you can take that flower, that love, with you to the next person, place, or activity.

Focus on one thing at a time. Do one thing at a time.

Make whatever you're doing right now, no matter what it is, the most important thing in your life.

SMALL THINGS DONE WITH GREAT LOVE

The art of love is mindfulness.

Mindfulness is just a moment of meditation. Meditation—
mindfulness—can be practiced all day, every day.

Meditation is not a position, posture, or mantra, and it doesn't require a special
time or place. It's not anything difficult, formal, or stuffy like that at all.

Meditation is simply the practice of being mindful; it's the practice of being present.

Whatever is done mindfully is done lovingly. Whatever is done
with nonjudgmental awareness is done with love.

Mother Theresa once said, "There are no great things.
There are only small things done with great love."

If something is done with love, it's right. If something
is done without love, it's wrong.

Love—nonjudgmental awareness—is the greatest spiritual quality
and the parent of all others. If you do anything, even the smallest
thing, with that kind of awareness, you're truly spiritual.

It's not *what* you do, but *how* you do it that counts.

If you do it with loving presence, it's right; without loving presence, it's wrong.

To experience true love, make the quality of each moment
more important than getting things done.

Just be aware of what is happening in the present moment. Just remain
conscious of what is happening in this moment, without judgment.

That present-minded, nonjudgmental awareness *is* love.

Love is just getting out of your own way so that your
natural state of love can surface again.

Love is just enjoying yourself without letting stressful,
judgmental thoughts get in the way.

BECOME A NOBODY

Meditation makes you a nobody.

Or, more accurately, meditation helps you *realize* that you—
and everybody else—are nobodies: "not bodies."

We are not our bodies, and we are not our minds, either.

We are not human beings having a spiritual experience—
we are spiritual beings having a human experience.

We are spirit. We are the one formless spirit that underlies all forms.

Meditation brings you to this realization. It brings
you to the realization of nothingness.

Of course, the nothingness of you as a body or mind is the everythingness of
you as spirit. The emptiness of you as the ego is the fullness of you as love!

In other words, when you become nothing—empty of lonely, loveless
thoughts; aware that you are not your lonely, loneliness thoughts—
love erupts within you. Suddenly, you are overflowing with love.

You (as the ego) are the host, and love is the guest. The guest
(love) only comes when the host (the ego) is gone.

When you are not, love is. When you are not lost in lonely
or loveless thoughts, love is your experience.

Love is losing yourself and finding yourself—losing your false sense
(the ego) and finding your true Self (spirit)—all in one breath.

A LIFETIME OF LOVE

Whenever you can, just enjoy yourself. Just enjoy
whatever you're doing without being distracted.

The practice of love is the practice of being joyful.

If you can do that—if you can learn to enjoy yourself, no matter what you
are doing—you will become aware of a great joy welling up inside you.

It is your own flowering, your own fragrance—that's joy.

When that joy arises, start sharing it with others—that's love.

Believe it or not, all the love you want is here now, in the
present moment. The future can't offer you anything more
than the present moment, no matter what it contains.

This tiny little moment, the one that's slipping between your
fingers right now, contains an entire lifetime of love.

•

LOVE IS AWARENESS

The foundation of love and happiness is awareness.

The basic condition for being happy is being *aware* of your being happy already; the
basic criterion for experiencing love is being *aware* of the love inside you already.

There is infinite love and happiness within you already,
but you have to be aware of it to enjoy it.

Just notice how full of love and happiness you are already, and you
will discover more love and happiness in no time, literally.

FINDING LOVE EVERYWHERE

Meditation is the root; love is the fruit.

Meditation is the root of love, and love is the fruit of meditation.

If you can understand this simple thing—if you can learn to slow down and enjoy each moment more—you will find love everywhere: in everything and everybody.

When you slow down and do things with joy, even trivial things become profound things. Even ordinary things become extraordinary things. Even small, insignificant things become significant, sacred things!

When you take your time and really focus on enjoying yourself, everything and everybody becomes another doorway through which you experience love.

If you really want to be in love, find a way to enjoy everything you do, no matter what it is. And if you can't enjoy it, try not to do it at all.

When you do anything with real joy, it automatically becomes loving. If you do it with real joy, you'll feel love even while doing the laundry or mowing the lawn. You'll feel love even while driving your car or going for a walk.

To me, joyful, nonjudgmental awareness is the greatest spiritual quality and the parent of all others. If you do anything, even the smallest thing, with that kind of awareness, you are truly spiritual.

When you are joyful, there is a tremendous, exploding, expanding energy inside of you. That energy is divine. That energy is love.

To find and feel love, live hotly! Do everything intensely and joyfully.

Enjoy what you do, no matter how big or small it is, and you will find yourself in love, inside and out.

BE WHOLE-HEARTED

Have you noticed?

A fetus is all heart. It is nothing but heart.

Even before a brain develops, a heart has already developed. And that heart is so big and beats with so much love that it is almost the fetus' entire being.

That's how I want you to be, too: full of love! I want you to be a big, throbbing heart. I want you to be full of life and love.

I want you to do everything wholeheartedly, with passion. I want you to do everything with real, heartfelt emotion, with your whole being.

Do everything from the heart, with all your heart, or don't do it at all.

Be whole-hearted—that's my encouragement.

•

THE ART OF LOVE

Practicing the art of love means being present.

It means being present while you're doing whatever you're doing.

It means to do whatever you're doing whole-heartedly. It means to do whatever you're doing with your undivided attention.

Practicing the art of love doesn't mean doing anything special or "spiritual." It just means living your ordinary life in an extraordinary way: with Presence.

It means being aware of what you're doing while you're doing it; it means remembering what you're doing while you're doing it.

It means not being distracted with a million and one other concerns. It means releasing all worries and plans, and just being right here with life.

Practicing the art of love is really practicing the Presence.

Chapter 8

LOVE IN EVERY BREATH

If you can learn to thoroughly enjoy a single breath,
you can find love right here and now.

In fact, you have found it already.

LOVE IN EVERY BREATH

Love is awareness.

And the first step of awareness is just this: "When breathing in, I'm aware that I'm breathing in. When breathing out, I'm aware that I'm breathing out. I remember what I'm doing while I'm doing it, and I let everything else go."

If you can breathe like this, you are practicing the art of love. You are experiencing true love, whether you know it or not.

In fact, if you can do anything with this kind of awareness, you can *feel* love anytime you want. You can be in love anytime and anywhere you want, no matter what else you're doing or with whom else you are doing it.

Just watch your breath without thinking so much. Just be aware of your breath without so much on your mind.

Remember your breath and let everything else go. Really be there and don't do anything else. Don't try to do anything special. Don't try to be spiritual.

Being in love—loving yourself and others—is the easiest, most natural thing in the world. Don't make it so hard. Keep it simple; don't complicate it.

Don't change your breathing; don't manipulate your breath. Don't try to take deep breaths, and don't try to take shallow breaths, either.

Just be natural, absolutely natural.

If your breaths are shallow, let them be shallow. If they are deep, let them be deep. Just experience them without trying to change them.

Just experience each breath without judging anything good or bad. Remember, judging is thinking, and thinking blocks true love.

Just relax and let your breathing be loose and natural. Let each breath come and go on its own, in its own good timing. Be there with each breath, with each moment.

This is the art of love: presence.

This is the secret to life and love: unconditional acceptance.

And even a single breath of life can teach it to you.

LOVE IS LIFE'S PRESENCE

Love means living in such a way that you are aware
of the love within you in every moment.

It means living in such a way that you are aware of love's presence—
God's presence, your presence—in every moment.

When you live in this way—with Presence—nothing more is needed.

You have it all.

•

LOVING LIFE WITH ALL YOUR MIND, HEART, AND SOUL

Jesus says, "Love God with all your heart and with
all your soul and with all your mind."

That's exactly what I mean, too.

Love life—the formless one life within you—with all your mind, heart, and soul.

To love is to enjoy. When you thoroughly enjoy anything, you are "loving it."

Love means unconditionally enjoying the life consciousness within
you, no matter what your outer life conditions contain.

It means enjoying the formless One Life within you
with all your mind, heart, and soul.

LOVING THIS BREATH UNCONDITIONALLY

Can you unconditionally love—enjoy—this moment?

Can you unconditionally love—enjoy—this breath?

Can you accept and appreciate this breath without asking it to be different?

Can you love this breath without judging, criticizing, or
condemning anything or anybody, including yourself?

Can you live, love, and enjoy this moment without fearing or desiring anything?

If you can, you've mastered the art of love.

If you can be aware of a single breath—if you can accept and appreciate
a single moment—without asking it to be different, there is nothing
more you need to learn. You have found true love already.

Now wash, rinse, and repeat.

Breathe... and become really alive! When you come alive, love will
come alive. When you are present, love will be present, too.

And lovers will show up everywhere. In fact, when love is
present, you are surrounded by nothing but lovers!

Remember, love isn't achieved—it's allowed!

Love isn't found—it's freed!

Love is what happens easily, effortlessly, and enjoyably when you
are just yourself. Love is what happens automatically when you're
relaxed and completely at ease with yourself and the world.

Rumi says, "Your task is not to seek for love, but merely to seek and
find all the barriers within yourself that you have built against it."

YOU ARE BEING BREATHED

When I say that "Presence is the answer," I don't mean that—simply by being present—you will always instantly feel peaceful, loving, and joyful.

I mean that, with Presence, everything else will happen on its own. You've started the ball rolling, and now the ball will roll on its own.

In time, you will experience deeper and deeper revelations, and those revelations will lead you to deeper and deeper experiences of love.

Of course, by "revelations," I mean "experiences."

I mean intuitive insights that result from direct, hands-on, personal experience. I *don't* mean abstract mental concepts or spiritual platitudes that result from intellectual thinking.

For instance, one of the revelations you might have is this: "I am not breathing—I'm being breathed!" That's a common one.

If you experience that revelation, it will help you to relax, and that relaxation will help you to fall deeper and deeper into love—the love that is inside you. It will help you to rise higher and higher in love—the love that you are.

That revelation will lead to deeper and deeper revelations, and there will be no end to those revelations. You will experience more and more love.

With increasing awareness, your insight will grow. With increasing insight, your joy will grow. With increasing joy, your love will blossom!

When you are tapped-in, tuned-in, and turned-on to Presence, a beautiful rhythm is revealed. You are in love! Now, even more revelations will reveal themselves to you.

For example, this revelation might reveal itself: "Breathing is not something I do—breathing is something that's done *to* me, done *for* me, and done *through* me, without my effort at all."

Then, perhaps, this little insight will follow: "Living isn't something I do—living is something that's done *to* me, done *for* me, and done *through* me, without my effort at all."

Next, this truth might be experienced: "I don't have a life—I *am* life! I can't lose my life, because I *am* life. I can't die, because life, by its very nature, is *always alive*. There really is nothing to fear!"

Then, this little nugget might be unearthed: "Love is not something I *do*—love is something that's done *to* me, done *for* me, and done *through* me, without my effort at all."

Finally, perhaps, the ultimate revelation is experienced: "Love—feeling love, being in love, *being* love—is as natural as breathing. To live is to love; to exist is to love. Love is natural. Love is just my natural state of felt oneness with life itself."

Suddenly, you are in love with life.

You are in love with this loving source that is breathing you, living you, and loving you. In fact, you *are* this loving source that is breathing *as* you, living *as* you, and loving *as* you.

You no longer feel separate—you feel one with all-that-is. In fact, it's more than that. You have disappeared completely, and all that's left is love!

We abide in life, and life abides in us. We abide *as* life, and life abides *as* us.

We live in love, and love lives in us. We live *as* love, and love lives *as* us.

The drop is in the ocean, but the ocean is in the drop, too!
The drop *is* the ocean, but the ocean *is* the drop, too!

When you no longer feel separate, love grows all by itself. When the illusion of separation drops, love arises naturally.

A person of meditation understands that there is no separation whatsoever. Separation is an illusion—only oneness is real.

Only life—and felt oneness with life—is real.

Only love is real.

THIS MOMENT IS YOUR LIFE

Love means knowing one thing:

This moment is all you have, so you have to make the most of it. Love means knowing that the next moment is not guaranteed to anybody.

When you know that this moment might be your last and that the next moment is not promised to anyone, you don't wait for love—you love! You don't wait for somebody to love you—you love yourself! You live each moment of life as though it's the last moment of your life.

Love is an understanding, the understanding that life is a gift you never earned. When you understand that, you can't not be grateful. You can't not feel loved, and you can't not love others.

When you understand that every moment of your life is a gift given out of God's grace—a gift given to you because life loves you so much—you can't possibly be anything other than truly, deeply grateful. When that understanding penetrates your heart—and not just your head—you can't possibly feel anything other than love.

When you understand that you are loved so much that you've been given—and continue to be given—life, which is the greatest gift of all, a feeling of deep gratitude grows in your heart.

That gratitude is love, true love.

Love is a heart beating with deep gratitude, because life is so good and being alive is so wonderful.

Every moment of your life is the most important moment of your life, because every moment of your life *is* your life. It's your *whole* life, your entire life.

It's the only moment that you can really live. It is the only time— although, it's really out of time, it's really timeless—where you can really be alive. It is the only moment that is ever in your hands.

My whole teaching is a teaching in how to be really alive, and being really alive means living in the moment. My whole effort is to get you to treat this moment—the only moment where life exists, the only moment where you can be alive—as though it really mattered.

People think that life consists of something called "the past," something called "the present," and something called "the future," but that's an illusion.

The past and the future are not part of life—the past and future are *apart* from life. The past and future aren't part of time—they are *apart* from time.

In other words, the past and future aren't part of time—the past and future are part of *mind*. They aren't reality—they are only *thoughts* about reality.

Life is always just one moment: *this* moment.

The past is a memory, and the future is a fantasy—only the present is reality.

The past and future are mind projections—only the present exists.

The present is the only place where real life and
love can be experienced and enjoyed.

To live with the awareness that you could "die"—and make your transition—
at any moment without even a single moment's notice is to live a life
of true love, a life in deep communion with life and all life forms.

The past is history, and the future is a mystery—only this moment is reality.

No past moment and no future moment can ever offer you anything
more than this precious, prosperous present moment.

In fact, only the present moment—only Presence
itself—can offer you anything at all.

And it offers it all! It offers everything you could ever possibly want or need.

INSTANT ENLIGHTENMENT

Instant coffee, instant breakfast, instant internet, instant access.

Why not instant enlightenment?

Enlightenment is the realization that we only have this moment to live. The next moment is uncertain—it may or may not come.

In fact, enlightenment is the realization that we only have (are) *Presence* itself. Nothing else is certain—everything else is uncertain.

In fact, nothing else exists at all in the way we think it does.

The secret of life is love, and the secret of love is not to think of yesterday, not to think of tomorrow, and not even to think of today.

The secret of love is not to think of any day, even today, but to live, love, and enjoy today.

Live here, wherever "here" is!

Love now, whatever "now" consists of!

Enjoy this, whatever "this" is!

To be enlightened is to be enlightened in the present moment. It's to enlighten yourself to this moment. Except for the enlightenment contained within the present moment, there is no other enlightenment in the whole world.

More accurately, to be enlightened is to be Presence itself.

It's to enlighten yourself to the Presence that you are right here and now. Except for the enlightenment that you are—the alive Presence that you are—there's no other enlightenment anywhere.

YOU ARE ENLIGHTENMENT

You don't become enlightened later.

You are enlightened now, only you don't know it.

In fact, you are enlightenment itself, but your over-analytical mind won't let you realize it. You are nothing but light, but your over-thinking mind won't let you see this fact.

Think about it: Except for humans, all of nature is enlightened. The trees, the rocks, the birds, the sun, and the moon are all enlightened.

It just means not to lose your (awareness of) Being in thinking. Instead, learn to lose your thinking in (awareness of) Being.

All of nature is enlightened, except human beings, because only human beings think incessantly. All of nature is living blissfully in the present moment, except for people, because only people are preoccupied with their own thoughts and feelings.

In other words, to be enlightened simply means not to think yourself out of enlightenment, the enlightenment that you already are. It means not to think so much that you no longer feel the peace, love, and happiness within you.

To be enlightened is to know that you *already* are enlightened—there is no other state. To be enlightened is but a recognition, not an achievement at all.

Enlightenment only has one requirement: being aware that you're enlightened already, that you are enlightenment itself.

Enlightenment only requires one thing: Being.

When you are just being—and not lost in thinking—you are enlightened, and you are *aware* that you are enlightened. You are enlightened to your pre-existing enlightenment, so to speak.

In other words, enlightenment just means to be more and think less.

Think less, be more!

Think less, live more.

Think less, love more.

Think less, enjoy more!

THE KEY TO ENLIGHTENMENT

More and more, notice when you are thinking. More and more, become aware of when you are lost in thought.

Just become aware; just notice—don't interfere or intervene.

Don't try to fix anything, don't try to get rid of anything, don't try to change anything, and don't try to replace anything with anything else.

Don't judge anything good or bad, don't condemn anything, and don't criticize anything.

Don't do anything—just *notice* everything. Just *observe* everything with nonjudgmental awareness.

Then, after practicing this for a while, you can eventually take the next step: Softly place your attention on attention itself. Direct your awareness to awareness itself. Just stand in, rest in, and abide as Awareness itself.

That's peace, love, and happiness.

And that's enlightenment, too.

NOTICING YOUR LACK OF PRESENCE...
IS PRESENCE

When you aren't present, just notice it.

Just become aware of the fact: "I'm not present. I'm missing
life, which is always this present moment."

No judgment, no guilt, no criticism, no condemnation.

In that very awareness, you have become aware again. By simply noticing that you
are not present, you instantly become present again. That noticing does all the work.

The moment you realize you are missing because you are brooding
too much, you start experiencing little openings or small gaps in
the traffic jam of your mind. Those gaps are moments of meditation,
moments of enlightenment, moments of true love.

You will become "enlightened," and you will become "unenlightened"
many times during the course of your life. You will remember that
you are enlightened—one with life and all life forms—and you will
forget that you are enlightened over and over again in your life.

In other words, you can do things in an enlightened way, or
you can do that same thing in an unenlightened way.

For instance, you can sip tea in an enlightened way, or you
can sip tea in an unenlightened way. You can sip tea with
Presence, or you can sip tea without Presence.

You can sip tea with an awareness of the peace, love, and joy within
you, or you can sip tea without an awareness of the peace, love, and
joy within you. You can sip tea in a peaceful, loving, and joyful way,
or you can sip tea in a stressful, unloving, and joyless way.

If you sip tea while thinking about something else, like what you are
going to do next, you are "unenlightened." It really is that simple.

The only thing that keeps you unenlightened—unaware of your preexisting
enlightenment, unaware of your oneness with life and all life forms,
unaware of how infinitely loved and loving you are—is thinking.

Too much thinking and not enough awareness.

LET YOUR SILENCE SING

Meditation is relaxation; to meditate is to relax.

When you meditate, you simply relax into yourself—the Self, God within.

When you relax, you become vulnerable. You open up.
You blossom, you bloom. You let the sunshine in.

That's called "experiencing the eternal sunshine of the spotless mind."

That's called "discovering the invincible summer within."

Albert Camus writes, "In the midst of winter, I found there was, within
me, an invincible summer. And that makes me happy. For it says that
no matter how hard the world pushes against me, within me, there's
something stronger—something better, pushing right back."

When you really relax, things start happening on their own.
Miracles start happening within you and all around you. That's
why people say, "Love is the greatest miracle on earth."

Meditation is a relaxed—but awake—mind.

It is listening silently to yourself, to other people, and to life itself with no tension
in your mind. It means listening to dogs barking, kids crying, sirens screaming,
emotions raging, and thoughts echoing with no tension in your mind at all.

It's perception without conception. It's sensation without explanation.
It's experiencing everything without explaining anything.

It's observing whatever happens—or doesn't happen—without identifying
with any of it or becoming overly involved with any of it. It's listening
to it all without an urge to know, learn, or control anything.

It is "letting go and letting God."

It is living, if only for a few moments, with no goal in mind at all.

Be silent—that's the first step.

Let your silence sing—that's the second step.

And two steps is the entire journey.

Chapter 9

GIVING & RECEIVING

Loving others is its own reward.

Giving is receiving.

TAKING RESPONSIBILITY

Nobody wants to take responsibility for the world's lack of love.

Nobody wants to take responsibility for the world's greediness, the world's hate, or the world's cruelty. Everybody wants to blame somebody else. But each of us is part of the world, so each of us is a part of the problem, too.

Consider your personal life: your friends and family. Consider your professional life: your clients, colleagues, and coworkers. When there are problems in your personal or professional life, everybody blames somebody else. Everybody thinks it is somebody else's fault—have you noticed?

Everybody thinks somebody else should be more loving. Everybody thinks the other person should be kinder, more caring, more generous, and more understanding. Nobody wants to be the one who should be more loving.

Everybody wants to be *loved*, but nobody wants to be *loving*. Everybody wants to *receive* love, but nobody wants to *give* love. Everybody wants to be the *beloved*, but nobody wants to be the *lover*.

Everybody wants to drink from the source of love, but nobody wants to *be* the source of love itself. Everybody wants to *get*, but nobody wants to *give*—isn't that the case?

The world is full of beggars—there I said it! The world is full of empty, bankrupt people. It is full of loveless people begging for love from other loveless people.

Everybody is waiting to get love from somebody else before they even think about giving it to anybody else.

That's backward. It never works.

To get love, you have to be the source of it yourself.

GIVE LOVE TO GET LOVE

It sounds counter-intuitive, but it's true:

You can't get love by withholding it. You have to *give* (be) love to *get* it. It is only by *giving* (being) love that you are able to guarantee the *receiving* of it.

It is only by *being love* that you can guarantee *being loved*.

However, please understand me: I'm not saying that, by giving love to Mary, Mary will return your love. I'm not saying that, by loving John, John will love you back.

No, the object of your affection won't always return your affection, but you'll receive love back, nonetheless—that's what I'm saying.

You don't necessarily get love back from the people to whom you've given it, but you get it back, nonetheless.

That's the miracle of love.

•

THE ARITHMETIC OF LOVE

When you start giving love, you start getting love back.

And the love you give doesn't just come back in equal proportions.

No, the love you give comes back to you in disproportionate sums! The love you give comes back a dozen-fold, a hundred-fold, a thousand-fold—it's exponential!

You don't necessarily get love back from the people to whom you've given it, but you get it back, nonetheless—that is the miracle of love.

Love is the only mathematics in the world that works this way: addition through subtraction, multiplication through division.

Love is the only arithmetic in the world that functions like this: The more you give, the more you get... and it's exponential!

DO IT FOR YOURSELF!

Love—being loving, *being* love—is something you
do for yourself, not for anybody else.

By being loving, you experience yourself as the *source* of love. When
you love somebody, you experience that love yourself, *first*.

Love is its own reward.

It's something you do for yourself, first and foremost,
because it feels so good to *you*.

•

YOUR LOVE LIFE IS IN YOUR HANDS

Your love life doesn't depend on anybody else, except you.

It depends on you and you only. It's completely in your hands, not anybody else's.

If you knew the secret of love, you could—you *would*—be in love all
day, every day. You could—you *would*—be in love 24/7, 365!

In truth, of course, being in love is your 24/7, 365 experience already, but
you don't know it, you aren't aware of it. So, you don't really feel it.

If you want love, it's up to you and you only.

This is good news. It means that it only takes one person
for you to be in love, and that one person is *you*.

LOVE AND THE LOVER WILL COME

Are you still waiting for a lover to show up before you start loving people?

Are you waiting for somebody to start loving you before
you start loving yourself or other people?

Do you have to wait for an audience before you start dancing, or
can you simply start dancing now? Do you have to wait for a sold-
out crowd before you start singing, or can you simply start singing
in the shower or the studio without the sold-out crowd?

If you wait for an audience before you start practicing your dance moves,
how will you ever attract an audience? If you wait for a sold-out crowd
before you start singing, how will you ever get a sold-out-crowd?

What's more, if you really love dancing, what does the audience have
to do with whether you dance or not? If you really enjoy singing, what
does a sold-out crowd have to do with whether you sing or not?

You don't need an audience to dance, sing, or celebrate your life, and
you don't need a lover before you start enjoying your love life. You
don't need a lover before you start loving. Can't you just start loving
yourself and other people for love's sake, for joy's sake alone?

The real thing in life is not *being loved* but *being loving*. The most
meaningful thing in life is not *finding* a lover but *being* a lover.

If you wait for a lover before you love, you might wait
an entire lifetime and never experience love.

Don't wait for a lover to love—love and the lover will come!

Finding a lover doesn't bring you love—you have to *be* a lover to find love.
You have to *be* love, first, and then everybody becomes your lover.

Love comes through you, not through anybody else.

Live now—don't wait!

Love now—don't procrastinate!

St. Augustine once said, "I am in love with loving."

That's how I feel, and that's how I want you to feel, too.

Be in love with loving!

A TALE OF TWO CITIES

Despite what you've heard, there are only two places to live in the world:

You can live in fear and separation or you can live in love and oneness. You can live as the empty, illusory ego or you can live as the real source of fullness and fulfillment within you.

You can live like a beggar in fear, or you can live like an emperor—like a Buddha—in love. You can live like a beggar in a shack of perceived lack and emptiness, or you can live like a king—like a Jesus—in a palace of true abundance and fulfillment.

You can live a beggarly life with the intent of *getting* something from the world—and both some materially poor people and some materially rich people live like this—or you can live a truly rich life with the intent of *giving* something to the world.

You can either live from the poor, poverty-stricken perspective of the ego, or you can live from the rich, prosperous perspective of Source.

When you live from the ego, you live in fear.

The ego means "Edging Good Out" or "Edging God Out." Naturally, you can't edge God (life) out, since you *are* God (life), but you can *think* you can.

The ego means "Everything Good Outside" or "Even God Outside." Of course, since you are one with the source of all good (God), God and everything good is always inside!

When you live in the non-ego, however, you live in love—in oneness with the source of life and love (God).

You live in God and God lives in you. You live, move, and have your being in Consciousness, Awareness, or Presence.

The question really is: Are you living like a beggar in fear and separation, or are you living like a king or queen in love and oneness? Are you living to get or are you living to give?

Take this book, for example. I haven't written this book or any other book to get something from the world. I've written this book to *give* something to the world.

With the ego, there is a desire to *get*; but with love, there is only a desire to *give*.

When you live from the ego, you want what you want because you think it will fulfill you. But when you live from love, you want what you want because you are fulfilled *already*. You are full already, and you simply want to share your overflow with the world!

This is why sometimes I say, "Love is a luxury. It is only for the rich!"

Love is only for the rich, the spiritually rich. It's only for those who are rich in peace, love, and joy. It's only for those who are rich in the presence, consciousness, or awareness of abundance within!

REAL WEALTH IS GIVING, NOT GETTING

You can only prove you are really rich by *giving*, not by *getting*.

People think that they can prove they are rich by having, but
you can never prove you are rich by having anything.

You are not really rich when you have *taken* something from the world.
You are only really rich when you have *given* something to the world.

There is no greater joy in the world than experiencing yourself as the source
of love. Sharing the love you found within yourself with the world is the
ultimate joy in life. It is its own reward—you don't expect anything in return.

When you share your love, you are simply grateful that you have something to
give. You are simply grateful for the opportunity to share your love with the world,
regardless of whether or not you have somebody "special" to share it with.

To a lover, *everybody* is special, and *nobody* is special, all at
the same time—the other person is just irrelevant.

What matters to a lover is *extending* his or her bliss to
others, not *extracting* his or her bliss from others.

What counts with a lover is being *loving*, not being *loved*. What
counts with a lover is being a *lover*, not being the *beloved*.

What's important to a lover is *relating*, not relationship.

When you have found the source of love within, loving others *is* the reward.

When you find the source of love within yourself, you don't care what anybody
else does with your love. You don't even care if the other person says, "Thank you."

You're just grateful that you had an opportunity to share
your love with somebody, with anybody. The joy that you feel
from giving your love away is "thank you" enough.

Don't love just to be loved. Don't love just to get love.

Love for love's sake. Love for joy's sake. Love for the joy of loving alone!

Unless you love the way a Jesus or a Buddha loves—for the pleasure of it alone—you can't really love at all.

Only a Jesus really loves—nobody else. Only a Buddha really loves—nobody else.

Only God—the God within you and me—really loves, nobody else.

SHARING WHAT YOU HAVE

When you *are* love, you share whatever you have without prompting, without encouragement, without a promise of reward, without a guarantee of results, and without an expectation of reciprocity.

When you *are* love, you're rich. You're rich in bliss. You're rich in an awareness of your oneness with the infinite, eternal source of everything. You're rich in the only real richness there is: Consciousness.

When you are love—when you know the source of infinite love is within you—you share that love in whatever form you can. If you don't share it, you're not yet part of the solution—you're part of the problem.

If you don't share, you're not really rich. You aren't really peaceful, loving, and joyful. You aren't really enlightened, Self-realized, or God-realized.

You have yet to arrive; you have yet to attain.

A person who *is* love knows one thing: "Death snatches everything away, so I should share what I have now. I should share what I have now, freely and joyfully, before it's snatched away from me forever!"

BE A GO-GIVER!

You can only give what you have.

Before you can give it, you have to have it to give.
Before you can give it, you have to get it.

But you can't get it from others. You can't get it from the world.

You have to get it from within, the source within you.

Get love, yes. Get love from the source within you, yes, but don't stop
there! Share that love you found within yourself with the world!

Remember: If you only get and never give, you'll live an empty life, a beggar's life.

Get love, yes, but *give* love, too.

Be a *go-getter*, yes, but be a *go-giver*, too!

Your purpose in life is to experience yourself as the source of everything you want.
Your purpose is to *get* love from the source, so that you can *give* love *as* the source.

Experience yourself as love, first.

Then, extend that love to the world!

THE LITMUS TEST FOR LOVE

It's easy to love people who love you.

The real challenge is to love people who *don't* love you or don't *seem* to love you. The real test is to love people you don't think are worth loving.

The real accomplishment is to love the unlovable.

Love has nothing to do with the other person—love only has to do with *you.* It has nothing to do with whether the other person deserves it or not. If the other person deserves your love, your love isn't worth very much, is it?

Anybody can love the lovable, but can you love the unlovable?

That's the real question.

It's not a question of anybody else's worthiness— it's only a question of your consciousness.

If you can love the unlovable, if you can forgive the unforgivable—if your heart is big enough, if your awareness is great enough—you will taste true love.

You already do.

Love isn't about anybody else being loveable—love is about you being love-able. It's about *you* being able or capable of loving all people, at all times, and under all conditions.

It's not about other people being lovable—it's about you *being* love.

NOW OR NEVER

Are you still waiting for a lover to love?

Please don't wait. With love, it's always now or never.

You don't need a lover to love—you can love the cashier,
the teller, the gardener, and the janitor.

You don't need somebody who loves you back—you can love your coworkers,
your boss, your ex-wife or ex-husband, and your mother-in-law.

You don't even need to love another human being—you can
love a lake, a tree, or a kitten. You don't need a person at all—
you can love the stars, the sunset, and the tulips!

Life is just this moment, that's all it ever is. If you want to experience true love,
you need to make the most of this moment, no matter what it contains.

When you make the most of this moment—when you live and love this moment
for what it contains, no matter what it contains—you experience happiness *now*.

That's the point of having a relationship or partner anyway, isn't it: happiness?

Plus, when you are happy now, you improve your capacity to love;
you improve your ability to love—your "love-ability."

When you experience happiness now, you become more "love-
able"—more capable of giving and receiving love.

In other words, when you enjoy this moment here and now, you
become happier. And when you become happier, you make your life—
especially your love life—better immediately, in at least two ways.

First, when you're happier, you become easier to love. You're
more fun to be around, so *you attract more lovers*.

Second, when you're happier, others become easier to love, too. The things that
other people think, say, and do don't bother you as much, so *more lovers attract you*.

It really is true: Happiness is attractive!

And it's also true: Happy people are better lovers!

FOR JOY'S SAKE

If you hold the door for somebody, and the person for whom
you held the door doesn't thank you, do you get upset?

If you let somebody pull out ahead of you in traffic, and the driver
whom you let out doesn't acknowledge you, do you get mad?

If you give money to a beggar on the street, and he doesn't seem
grateful to you, do you resent having given him that money?

If you do something kind for another person, and that person doesn't
reciprocate your kindness, do you feel taken advantage of?

If you love your partner, and he or she cheats on
you, do you feel angry, jealous, or sad?

If you love another man or woman, but your love is unrequited,
do you feel unhappy, embarrassed, or ashamed?

If you've been "a good person" for most of your life, and you have little to
show for it, are you angry with the world, life, or God? Are you possibly
even considering a different, less loving way of life altogether?

This isn't real love. Real love is more selfish than that!

Real love loves for its own sake, for joy's sake alone!

ALWAYS IN LOVE

When you love somebody, you're really loving yourself.

Only you don't know it.

When you love that way—when you love for love's sake, when you love for joy's sake alone—you are in love at all times, in all places, and with all people.

When you love people in this way, you exist in a state of love.

You *are* love.

Then, no matter what anybody else does with that love, you live a life of love. You're always in love, partner or not.

When you *are* love, it doesn't matter if anybody else accepts or appreciates your love. It doesn't matter if anybody returns your love. When you love people without expecting anything in return, you are always in love, and nobody can bring you out of it.

When you love simply because it feels so good to you, having a relationship or partner becomes much less important to you, because everybody has become your partner. Everybody has entered into a relationship with you, whether they know it or not!

Then, from this place, attracting a partner happens much more easily and effortlessly.

You are the source of love, and the source of love is infinite. No matter how much or how little love you get from anybody else in the world, it's never a problem, because there's always more where that came from!

Despite popular opinion, we are not just here to *get* love—we are here to *give* it, too. We are not just here to *receive* love—we are here to *extend* it, too. We are here to experience ourselves as the source, the only true source of love in the world.

When you experience yourself as the source of love, you will never be lonely again. When you become love—when you become aware that you *are* love—you begin a lifelong love affair with yourself that never ends.

LOVE YOUR NEIGHBOR AS YOURSELF

This Bible says, "Love your neighbor as yourself."

Indeed, whether you like it or not, you *always* love your neighbor as yourself.

This is true for two reasons.

First, you can *only* love your neighbor as much as you love yourself. If you don't love yourself, you can't love your neighbor—you have nothing to give!

Second, when you love your neighbor—or anybody, for that matter—you are, in effect, loving *yourself*. When you love anybody else, *you* feel the benefits of that love, first!

Always remember: When you hate anybody, you are hating *yourself*, because you are making happiness *impossible* for yourself. Likewise, when you love anybody, you are loving *yourself*, because you are making happiness *possible* for yourself.

"Love your neighbor as yourself" is not just a religious commandment—it's a spiritual truth.

Whether we like it or not, we always love or hate our neighbors as ourselves—we have no other choice. That's the nature of things.

You *are* your neighbor—that's the truth.

We are all one—that's true wisdom and real love.

UNCONDITIONALLY HAPPY, UNCONDITIONALLY LOVING

Here's a reminder:

Only unconditionally happy people are capable of
being unconditionally loving people.

Here's why: An unconditionally happy person doesn't waste any
time being unhappy or unloving for any reason whatsoever.

She doesn't waste any time or energy being unhappy or unloving
toward anybody, for any reason, however justified.

When you're unconditionally happy, love flows from you like a
fountain; it follows you like a shadow—you can't escape it!

In other words, everybody in the world, friend or foe, represents yet
another opportunity to be happy, because everybody represents another
opportunity for you to experience yourself as the source of love itself.

And experiencing yourself as the *source* of love *is* happiness;
experiencing yourself as the *source* of happiness is love.

In other words, loving other people is selfish—it's something
you do for *yourself*, because it feels so good to *you*!

GIVING IS RECEIVING

Every morning I go for a run.

Occasionally, on my run, I pass a homeless man on the street. He's not your typical homeless man. This man is full of light and love. To look into this man's eyes is to feel deep compassion, real joy, and true love. Can you imagine?

This man—Black, homeless, hungry, alone, with a catheter running down his leg—is concerned for me. That is the feeling he communicates through a single glance. Can you even fathom that? To look into this man is to see the divine.

When I have anything at all—whether it's a few coins or a few twenties—I give it to this man. I don't care what he does with it. I don't care if he buys food or drugs or alcohol. To simply see this man and be with this man for a few seconds is enough, more than enough.

To be with this man is to be with the divine. Do you understand that? What he has given me is so much and what I have given him is so little. It doesn't even compare. What I've given him is so paltry, so small: a few dirty pieces of scrap metal and a few filthy green bills with some old faces on it.

But what he's given me is so incredibly rare and precious: a taste of love, an experience of the divine. The two don't even compare. In what world does this exchange seem like a good bargain, a fair trade? On no planet would this little trade be just.

And yet, he has no complaints, not a single complaint. He looks at me with such deep gratitude, such love, such genuine heartfelt thanks. That man has penetrated me. He has penetrated me with that gratitude. He looks at that little bit of paper that I gave him as though it were diamonds. His eyes, his vision transforms everything into something blissful and beautiful, into something divine!

He has never asked me for a single thing. Not once. He has not asked—and there is certainly nothing wrong with asking—but he has not even asked me for a dime.

And that is the only way to give—not me, him! The way this man gives—out of his richness, out of his overflowing bliss—is the only way to give. When you give like this, like my friend, it is such bliss that you cannot even imagine. When you see a man like this, you must ask yourself: "Who is really the beggar here?" Surely, it is not him!

Around Christmas time, I had some extra money. Immediately, I went in search of this man—my friend. I searched high and wide, but I could not find him anywhere. I had a plane home to catch so that I could be with my family for the holidays. I was already running late, my bags weren't fully packed, and the ride to the airport was waiting. Nonetheless, I circled block after block looking for this man. I never found him.

To this day, I don't know where he went. I don't know where he is. Every day, like clockwork, he was on that corner, and then, on the most important day of all days, he was missing. He was nowhere to be found.

I went home, gathered my stuff for the airport, and set off for my trip. I was disappointed, very disappointed. When I could finally be helpful to this man in a big, material way, I couldn't find him.

An opportunity was missed—not by him, but by me! He didn't just miss an opportunity—I missed an opportunity, too. I missed an even greater opportunity than him; I missed the opportunity to *receive* a tremendous gift: the gift of *giving*.

Please always remember: giving is one of the greatest gifts you can ever receive.

LOVE YOURSELF AND LOVE OTHERS, TOO

If you don't love yourself, you can't love others.

But, also, if you don't love others, you haven't yet attained. You haven't realized the primary purpose of your life: felt oneness with life itself.

True love.

If you don't love yourself, you can't love others. But if you don't love others, your life lacks meaning.

•

THREE STAGES OF LOVE

There are three stages of love.

The first stage is "ego evaporating."

That's emptiness. That's clearing out the ego. That's seeing through the rain and fog of the illusory ego. That's "meditation."

The second stage is "joy arising."

That's fullness. That's inviting in—or realizing you are always one with—the divine. That's "joy."

The third stage is "love showering."

That's overflow. That's sharing the joy you found in meditation with the world. That's "love."

Ego evaporating, joy arising, love showering—those are the three stages of love.

LOVE-ABLE

Your love life doesn't depend on anybody else loving you.

Your love life only depends on you loving yourself.

In other words, your love life does not depend on anybody else being lovable—your love life only depends on you being "love-able."

Being "love-able" means being *"able to love."*

Being "love-able," in the way that I mean it, is not about getting other people to love you.

Being "love-able" is about getting *you* to love *yourself* enough that *you* can easily, effortlessly, and enjoyably love other people—*all* other people.

Being "love-able" means being able to love people—*all* people—regardless of who they are, what they think, what they say, or what they do.

•

LOVE: GIVING BIRTH TO A BUNDLE OF JOY

Giving birth to love is like giving birth to a baby.

Prior to conception, you are just an empty womb. You are ready, waiting, and willing, but you are barren.

That's the first phase of love: emptiness.

When you conceive, you have a bundle of joy inside! That bundle of joy inside can't be expressed, but he or she also can't be fully hidden.

That's the second phase of love: fullness.

When you give birth, you are ready to share that bundle of joy inside you with the world. You can't contain it any longer. You simply have to let that bundle of joy out—that's love!

That's the final phase of love: overflow.

Love is simple when you understand it.

LOVE AND NURSING

Love is like nursing a baby.

Here's why: The more you give, the more you have. And
the more you have, the more you can give.

The source of milk is constantly replenishing itself so that it has more and more
to give. If you don't give—if you don't share what you have—you will lose it.

The miracle of love works in exactly the same way: The more you give,
the more you get. The more you share, the more you have to share. If
you don't give—if you don't share what you have—you will lose it.

Buddha is right, "You only lose what you cling to."

Clinging means losing. If you keep your love to yourself, you lose it.

You only get to keep what you give away. When you
give it away, you get more to give away.

That's what happens when a woman nurses her baby, and
that's what happens when a human being loves.

In other words, to be filled with love, you must empty yourself.
To be fulfilled, you must share what you have.

Don't wait—share what you have now!

Don't prepare to love—love now!

Don't save any love for a later date. Don't save any joy for a special
occasion. *Today* is a special occasion. *Today* is cause for celebration.

Don't wait—use it all up now!

The well will never run dry. Life—source itself—will
feed you, sustain you, and provide for you.

However, you must do your part: You must trust.

LOVE AND NURSING (2)

In other words, in love and nursing, the key is to share what you have. But to share what you have, you must make sure you have it to share, first.

To give, you must get, first.

In nursing, that means to sleep and eat, first—then, feed your baby. Rest, refresh yourself, and replenish yourself, first—then, share that refreshment and replenishment with your baby.

Nursing, like love, is a pendulum. A pendulum swings from one side to the other. If you allow the pendulum to get stuck to one side or the other, the pendulum is no longer a working pendulum. It is no longer a functioning mechanism.

For instance, if you constantly only nurse—but never sleep or eat—you will not be able to sustain your nursing. Your milk won't last, because *you* won't last.

On the other hand, if you only sleep and eat—but don't nurse—you are withholding a great joy from yourself and from your baby. If you don't nurse, you can develop an infection, like mastitis, and that infection can make you sick.

Jesus says, "If you bring forth what is within you, what you bring forth will save you. If you do not bring forth what is within you, what you do not bring forth will destroy you.

In other words, love yourself, so that you can love other people. Love yourself, but don't stop there—love other people, too!

If only you'd give, you'd have! Just give and you'll have it to give!

Chapter 10

NON-JUDGMENT & NON-ATTACHMENT

Love is happiness.

And happiness doesn't judge.

That's how it remains happy… and loving

NO GUARANTEES

The world often mistakes attachment for love, but attachment is not love.

Attachment is the only thing that *gets in the way* of love.

Attachment is anti-love; attachment is the *absence* of love.

Attachment is really fear.

In other words, through attachment, people look for guarantees in the world, but the world offers no such guarantees. The world, by its very nature, is insecure.

To live in a 100 percent "secure" world, you would have to live in an imaginary world, and to have a 100 percent "secure" relationship, you would have to be with an imaginary person... or a dead one.

Face it: If security is what you want in this life, only a graveyard will do.

Unfortunately, many relationships have become exactly that: dead. They have become nothing more than steel-clad business contracts signed by two, security-seeking individuals.

Most people live physically, until they are seventy years of age, but die inside, at the age thirty. Most people live the majority of their lives as breathing corpses—have you noticed?

You live, but are you really alive?

THE SOURCE OF ALL SUFFERING

The cause of every relationship problem in the world is in the mind.

Relationship problems only exist in the mind. In the humble harmony of our hearts and in the silent serenity of our souls, we are all the same: We are all love.

The happiest relationships consist of two happy hearts, not two identical minds. The happiest relationships consist of two happy people, not two people who always agree with each other about everything.

Relationship problems happen not because people think different thoughts, but because people take their different thoughts seriously.

If people could learn to take their thoughts less seriously—if they could be less attached to their thoughts; if they could recognize that they were thinking thoughts and not reality; if they could stop believing all of their thoughts—peace, love, and joy would prevail.

Notice how many people are willing to sacrifice the things that matter most—peace, love, happiness, health, and so on—for a thought, opinion, judgment, or belief in their head. Notice how many people are even willing to die for what they think or believe.

Notice how many wars are fought over thoughts, how many people are willing to go to war—war with themselves, war with their family and friends, and war with the world—over a difference of opinion or belief.

The most painful moments in life and relationships occur when (1) your head is full of stressful thoughts, and (2) you believe—or take seriously—those stressful thoughts.

When you believe or take a thought seriously, it's called an "'attachment." Anytime anything disturbs your peace of mind, it's called an attachment, because you are attached to a story.

The most painful moments in life and relationships, then, occur when your head is full of *attachments to* stressful thoughts, instead of nonjudgmental *awareness of* those stressful thoughts.

No matter what you think you need in the world, all you really need is the ability to stop believing in—and taking seriously—stressful thoughts. Non-attachment is that ability. It's the ability to stop believing in, taking seriously, and being attached to stressful thoughts.

Peace, love, and joy are experienced when you let go of your attachment to what you think, no matter what you think.

FREEDOM FROM ATTACHMENT

Love is freedom, and freedom is non-attachment.

To love people, you have to give them freedom. And when you give others freedom, you give yourself the same freedom. When you let others off the hook, you let yourself off the hook, too.

When you let others out of prison—out of that little, self-created prison of what you believe they should think, say, and do—you quit your job as prison guard altogether.

That's a win-win, in my book.

That's freedom, and that freedom is happiness.

In other words, to love people properly, you have to be unconditionally happy. And to be unconditionally happy, you have to completely drop your attachment to how you think anybody or anything should be.

If you're attached—if you attach your *happiness*—to what anybody else thinks, says, or does, you can't be unconditionally happy. And if you can't be unconditionally happy, you can't be unconditionally loving. You're not free to love people as they are now; you've now placed conditions on your love and happiness.

All attachment says, "I can only be happy *if...* I can only love them *if...*"

Do you see how that hinders your experience of happiness?
Do you see how that limits your experience of love?

That's *conditional* happiness, and conditional happiness is not happiness at all. That's *conditional* love, and conditional love is not love at all.

Sometimes people think that attachment—attaching your love and happiness to how a person thinks, speaks, and acts—means loving them more. And they think that non-attachment—giving people freedom to think, speak, and act in whatever way they want—means loving them less.

But that is simply not true!

The truth is that, without the fetter of attachment,
you are free to love people *more*, not less.

When your happiness isn't tied to anybody or anything being a certain way, you're free to be as happy as you want. And when you're free to be as happy as you want, you're free to be as loving as you want, too. There's no longer anything at stake; your love and happiness are not on the line.

Love and happiness are *always* an open hand, open heart, and open mind—never a closed fist, closed heart, or closed mind.

LOVE, ATTACHMENT, AND SURRENDER

Dropping your attachments doesn't mean you have to divorce your spouse, break up with your significant other, unfriend your friends, disown your family, sell your house, quit your job, or be a doormat for other people.

Dropping your attachments just means that you stop letting your happiness depend on anybody or anything outside of you. It means you start making your happiness depend on you and you only.

In other words, then, you don't have to renounce your possessions—you just have to renounce possessiveness. You just have to renounce your materialistic attitude. You just have to renounce your unhealthy attachment to your possessions.

You don't have to quit your job—you just have to quit your unhealthy *attachment* to your job. You just have to quit stressing about your job.

You don't have to disown your family—you just have to disown your unhealthy *attachment* to your family. You just have to disown the need for your family to accept and approve of you.

You don't have to abandon your opinions and beliefs—you just have to abandon your unhealthy *attachment* to your opinions and beliefs. You just have to give up your need for anybody else to see the world in the same way you do.

You don't have to drop anything—you just have to drop your *attachment* to everything!

Dropping your attachments means giving up what-should-be for what-is. It means letting go of what you think life and people should be, so that you can experience and enjoy life and people as they really are.

Dropping your attachments means removing all the hurdles you've put in the way of your happiness; it means removing all the limitations you've put on your love life.

Believe it or not, reality is always sweeter than fantasy. Life is always better than your thoughts about it.

Without attachments, reality is nirvana already.

It is blissful already.

Byron Katie says, "God is reality, because reality rules."

When you stop arguing with reality and accept what-is, you surrender your will to divine will. You let go of what you think life *should* be doing and let in what life *is actually* doing.

Let go and let God. It's the only way to be happy, and it's the only way to stay in love.

Again, this doesn't mean that you should stay in an unhealthy relationship, keep a miserable job, continue hanging out with a Negative Nelly, keep useless possessions, or live in a shabby place.

It just means that, while you work on making your way out of those undesirable circumstances, whatever they might be, you make the best of it in the meantime.

If you have to take the ride anyway, you might as well enjoy it as much as you can.

LOVE IS LIKE FRESH AIR

Love is like fresh air.

Like air, love only remains fresh if it remains *free*.

Just imagine what would happen if people treated fresh air like love. Imagine if people—in their fear that fresh air would escape the house—shut all their windows and closed all their doors.

What would become of the fresh air? Well, the air would quickly lose its freshness and become stale!

This is exactly what people do with love.

Fearing that the love will escape their relationship, people shut all their windows and close all their doors. They try to seal in each other's love. They try to create a guarantee, a safeguard, for love.

However, in their attempt to secure, lock-in, and guarantee a fresh, loving experience, they only kill the love—and often the relationship, too—in the process, instead.

It's interesting, isn't it? *The things we do to stay alive end up killing us, and the things we do to keep love alive end up killing it.*

Always remember: *Things only remain fresh if they remain free!*

When love is no longer free, it is no longer fresh. When love is no longer free, it is no longer happy. In fact, it is no longer love at all!

Suddenly, you're in a relationship with a slave, not a partner; suddenly, you're in a relationship with a dictator, not a lover.

When love isn't free, saying "no" becomes impossible. And when saying "no" becomes impossible, saying "yes" becomes meaningless.

When love is full of attachments, it becomes an obligation, a duty, and a burden.

That is not love at all.

THE HIGHEST VALUE

Love is freedom.

In fact, I'd like to say that freedom is an even higher value than
love, because without freedom, love is not possible.

If you truly love somebody, you want them to be happy. That's really what love is: a
desire for the other person to be happy, even if that means them not being with you.

It's a hard pill to swallow, but it's the truth, nonetheless.

If you truly love somebody, you have to set that person free
to be themself, completely and unapologetically.

In other words, if you want to be happy, and you want others to
be happy, you have to drop your attachment to what you think
anybody else should be thinking, saying, or doing, period.

You can't control other people, so your attempt to control anybody
else only makes you both more and more frustrated. And the more
frustrated you both are, the less happy you both are. And the less happy
you both are, the less loving you both can be toward each other.

Without attachments and attempting to control each other, people
worry that the other person might leave them. Believe it or not,
however, it's actually your attachments and attempts at impossible
control that often *cause* the other person to leave you.

Your attachments and attempts at impossible control don't prevent people
from leaving you—they precipitate people leaving you! They make people
want to leave you *more*; they give people more reasons to leave you.

So, please don't worry about whether anybody will be with you tomorrow.
Understand that they might not be—then, enjoy their company while you have it.

If you do that, people will be much more likely to stick around.

LOVE IS NON-JUDGMENT

Love is non-judgment, complete non-judgment.

No expectations, no complaints, no desire to change,
and no desire to keep the same, either.

Love is acceptance, complete acceptance.

Light and darkness have never met. Never have, never will. They've
never even heard of each other. Likewise, love and judgment have never
met. Never have, never will. No introduction is ever possible.

Judgement is the absence of love, just as darkness is the absence of light. When
light enters, all darkness disappears; and when love enters, all judgment disappears.
If judgment doesn't leave when love enters, please know it's not real love.

Drop the judgment and let the love in already!

•

LOVE IS BLIND

Love is blind, but not for the reasons people think it is.

"Love is blind" doesn't mean that love is ignorant.

Love isn't ignorant—love is intelligent. Love is divine
wisdom. It is the peak of spiritual awareness.

Love isn't ignorant—love is *innocent*. Love is a state of non-
judgment; love doesn't judge. It doesn't condemn.

Love just loves—indiscriminately and unconditionally.

Love is blind, because love doesn't discriminate or judge.
If love discriminates or judges, it's not real love.

THE ONLY DISCIPLINE

Truly loving people don't try to control anybody or anything.

They don't try to control anything—they just try to *understand* everything.

They become more meditative, watchful, and observant. They observe their thoughts, feelings and behaviors. They try to understand what is there.

Of course, by "understand," I don't mean think about, examine, analyze, or intellectualize. I mean *observe without judgment.* I mean observe until understanding develops on its own.

What you understand, you transcend. When understanding deepens, transcendence arises. Understanding is transcendent; it's transformative.

To understand anything, just become a witness. In that witnessing, the sun rises, the ice melts, and the water evaporates completely.

In that witnessing, love arises, fear melts, and the ego—judgment and attachment—evaporates completely. The coldness—the non-peace, non-joy, and non-love within you—dissolves and disappears completely.

The poison—the hate, greed, jealousy, anger, misery, and frustration—is alchemically transmuted into honey, into something sweet and nutritious.

That's what Buddha says, that's what I've experienced, and that's what you can experience, too. Your hate, your anger, your greed, your jealousy, your possessiveness—it all becomes love.

Just watch: Miracles will happen within you and all around you. To watch, you have to be aware, nonjudgmentally aware.

Don't say, "This is right, this is wrong. This is good, this is evil. This will lead to heaven, this will lead to hell."

Don't judge—positively *or* negatively.

Just live in nonjudgmental awareness. Just live as loving awareness.

Just live *as* love.

DROPPING JUDGMENT

To stop judging, don't resist, deny, or fight your judgmental thoughts.

That doesn't work.

To stop judging, simply become *aware* of your judgmental thoughts.
Just non-judgmentally observe your judgmental thoughts. The key
is to use thoughtless awareness, not more analytical thinking.

Believe it or not, the mind can't be nonjudgmental. Only
by going *beyond* the mind—only by watching the mind with
nonjudgmental awareness—can you be nonjudgmental.

Only through meditation—observing the mind with dispassionate
detachment—can you become nonjudgmental.

For one week, try this: Keep a journal of every judgment you
make. Write down every judgment you make of yourself, of
other people, of the world, of life itself, and of God.

Record all of it, but do so without judging those judgments,
without trying to change those judgments in any way, and
without trying to get rid of those judgments whatsoever.

You'll be surprised—even the least judgmental people are highly judgmental.

It doesn't matter if you're judging others, judging yourself,
or judging life itself. At the end of the day, all judgment is
misery, and all judgment leads to even more misery.

The only way to end that misery is to introduce nonjudgmental awareness. The only
way to end that misery is to rest, relax, and abide as nonjudgmental awareness.

The only way is to rest in (and as) love itself.

Remember: You can't always instantly stop thinking judgmental thoughts, but
you can become more *aware* of those judgmental thoughts when you're thinking
them. In that awareness, the judgment begins to disappear all by itself.

Awareness—nonjudgmental awareness of judgmental
thoughts—is the only thing that can save you.

In other words, all people are judgmental—only Awareness, Consciousness, or Presence is really nonjudgmental. 'Only God within is good.' Only God is love.

We are all judgmental people. The difference is that some of us believe those judgemental thoughts, and some of us don't believe those judgemental thoughts. Some of us take those judgmental thoughts seriously, and some of us don't take those judgmental thoughts seriously.

Some of us think those judgments are reality, and some of us know better. Some of us know those thoughts are just thoughts. They don't mean anything unless we say they do, unless we give them meaning.

Just become aware of your judgmental thoughts without judging them, without adding an additional layer or level of suffering to it all.

In time, they'll start leaving you alone.

THE ONLY VIRTUE

I don't teach self-discipline, self-control, or self-improvement.

I teach Self-acceptance, Self-awareness, and Self-abidance.

I don't teach right and wrong—I teach nonjudgmental awareness.

That which is done with nonjudgmental awareness is right, and that which is done without nonjudgmental awareness is wrong.

Awareness makes clear to you what is right and wrong.

Some things can only be done *with* awareness—those things are right. Other things can only be done *without* awareness—those things are wrong.

Awareness helps you know what you should and shouldn't do. It helps you know whether or not something will bring you peace, love, and joy.

Like an athlete, when you are in the zone—present,
aware—the right action arises naturally.

St. Augustine says it this way, "Love and do what you will."

When you're full of loving non-judgmental awareness—when you are present, when you are aware of Presence—everything falls into place on its own.

Awareness is the only virtue.

Only Presence is good.

"Only God (within) is good."

THE ONLY VIRTUE (2)

Love is a perceptual shift from unawareness to awareness; from unconsciousness to consciousness; from ego to non-ego; from fear to non-fear; from illusion to reality; from separation to oneness; from hell to heaven.

Love will save you from hell—the hell inside you, the hell of self-judgment; the hell of fear and guilt; the feeling that you are separate from anybody or anything in the world.

In other words, love is the greatest virtue and the parent of all others, and ego is the greatest vice and the parent of all others.

Love is the only virtue.

Ego is the only vice.

Chapter 11

COMMUNICATION & COMMUNION

Love is not two minds in agreement—love is two hearts in alignment.

Love is not two minds meeting—love is two hearts melting.

Really, love is the recognition that all hearts
are already merged in The One.

THE HAPPIEST RELATIONSHIPS

The happiest relationships don't consist of two minds
that are always in agreement with each other.

The happiest relationships consist of two hearts that are
consistently in alignment with each other.

In other words, the happiest relationships consist of two happy people
who know that there's more to life than what they think about.

The happiest relationships consist of two people who know
that disagreements are healthy, human, and inevitable, but that
arguments are silly, stupid, and completely avoidable.

*In other words, the happiest relationships consist of two people
who know how to disagree without being disagreeable.*

HEART-TO-HEART COMMUNICATION

Love is simple.

Love means letting go of everything that's in the way of love so that you can experience it for yourself. It means letting go of everything you think you know so that you can experience a deeper, more fulfilling love, first-hand.

Remember, love doesn't live in your head—love lives in your heart. Love means living from your heart, not your head.

Love means letting go of your attachment to all mental positions—all opinions, beliefs, and perspectives—so that you can manifest your true nature: love.

It means coming from a more peaceful, loving, and joyful place so that you can communicate with everybody in a more peaceful, loving, and joyful way.

Love means communicating with everybody through your heart, instead of your head.

Contrary to popular opinion, communication alone won't improve a relationship. Head-to-head communication alone won't improve a relationship.

Only *heart-to-heart* communication will improve a relationship.

Erich Fromm says, "Love is possible only if two persons communicate with each other from the center of their existence."

The center of your existence is your heart, your spiritual heart.

Your spiritual heart is still and silent. In fact, your spiritual heart is stillness and silence itself.

As such, it can only be accessed through non-thinking—not through thinking. It can only be accessed through thoughtless awareness.

It can only be accessed through silence.

A TERRIBLE MASTER,
BUT A WONDERFUL SERVANT

Please don't misunderstand me.

Despite my focus on the heart, please don't think that I want you to get rid of your mind. The mind is very useful; it is very valuable. It is absolutely necessary in this life.

However, your mind's chatter should never be allowed to drown out your heart's voice. The head's logic should never be allowed to replace the heart's love. Logic is no substitute for love.

The head and heart should work together, in simpatico. They should complement each other.

In fact, if you want to live a life of peace, love, and joy, the heart should take precedence; it should take priority. The heart should always lead, and the head should always follow.

To live a life of peace, love, and joy, the heart should always be the master. The heart should give the orders, and the head should follow behind, carrying out those orders, intelligently and obediently. That's the only way to live a peaceful, loving, and joyful life.

In other words, "The mind is a terrible master, but a wonderful servant."

When you get this wrong, when you have this backward—when the head is the master and the heart is the servant—chaos, conflict, and confusion ensue. Peace, love, and joy become impossible.

Sigmund Freud said, "[If the mind is the master...] intelligence will be in the service of neurosis."

If the mind is the master, intelligence will be in the service of madness. It will be in the service of mental illness. It will be in the service of fear, because that's all the mind knows.

However, if the heart is the master, intelligence will be in the service of sanity. It will be in the service of spiritual health. It will be in the service of love, because that's all the heart, the spiritual heart, knows. That's all the soul knows. That's all God knows.

The practice of putting the mind aside and letting the heart lead is the practice of love.

Quiet your mind and listen to your heart, your spiritual heart.

It knows best.

FOLLOW YOUR HEART

Love means following your heart.

It means listening to your spiritual heart, your soul, God within.

Always listen to your heart. Always follow your own nature. Always listen
to your own being. Seek your own counsel. Make your own decisions.
Only you know what's best for you. Listen to your heart and follow it.

Sure, you might go astray. But unless you go astray,
how will you ever know the right way?

Sure, you might knock on many wrong doors. But it's only by knocking on many
wrong doors that you will ever be able to recognize the right door when you find it.

Sure, you might fall down many times. But it's by falling down and
getting up that you build strength, the strength you need to succeed!

Listen to your heart—your spiritual heart, your soul, God
within—and follow it, unfailingly and unflinchingly.

To listen to your heart, however, you have to quiet your mind.

The mind knows little, but it shouts loudly. The heart knows much, but
it speaks only in a whisper. When you want to know something, like
what to do or where to go, quiet your mind and listen to your heart.

That's what meditation is: It is the art of listening to your heart.

And that's what prayer is, too: It is listening to the still, small voice within.

Quiet your mind, so that you can notice what naturally
uplifts you. When you find it, surrender to it.

MADNESS OR MEDITATION?

There are two paths in life: mind or no-mind.

There are two approaches to life: madness or meditation.

Mind is madness; to live in the mind is madness.

No-mind is meditation; to live in no-mind is mysticism.

To live in your head is to be mad, no matter how many people live that way.

But to live from your heart is to be free and enlightened,
no matter how many people *don't* live that way.

The kind of love that I'm talking about doesn't come
from the head—it comes from the heart.

It doesn't come from the mind—it comes from no-mind.

It comes from meditation.

•

MEDITATE... THEN, RELATE!

In other words, if you want to experience true love, forget all about love.

Instead, go deeply into meditation. Love is the outcome,
the result, the fragrance of meditation.

It's only your mind that ever blocks your experience of love. It's only
too much thinking that ever gets in the way of you experiencing the
invincible summer within, the eternal sunshine of the spotless mind.

In other words, true love is born out of stillness and silence.

Love born out of the body is lust or sex; love born out of the mind
is infatuation or attachment; and love born out of the spiritual heart
or soul—born out of silence and meditation—is true love.

Meditate.

Then, relate.

That's what I'm saying.

NAMASTE

I've always loved the term, "Namaste."

"Namaste" means, "I honor that place within you where—if you are in that place within you, and I am in that place within me—there is only One of us. There is a sacred place within each of us, where—when you are in yours and I am in mine—there is only One of us."

There is only life (God) and felt oneness with life (love).

That sacred place is your heart, not your head. When you're living from your heart—and not from your head—heart-to-heart communication happens effortlessly. The more you live from your heart, the better you express your true, loving nature.

In fact, to call this type of relating "communication" is not quite right. It is not communication—it is *communion*. When you connect with another living creature on a heart-to-heart level, you are not just communicating—you are communing.

You are making love, so to speak; it is the highest form of making love.

When you communicate—when you commune—in this way, you are full of loving awareness. When you communicate or commune from that place of loving awareness, you are inspired—you are "in spirit."

You are in God, and God is in you... and you know it. You are in love, and love is in you... and you know it.

When you are in God's love, and God's love is in you—when you know that you *are* God, and God *is* you—it isn't communication at all.

It is communion with the All.

You aren't just saying something with your words—you are saying something with your heart and soul. You are saying something with your entire being!

To *communicate* is to say something with your head, but to *commune* is to say something with your heart and soul.

When you *are* love, you are in conscious communion with—felt oneness with—All-That-Is. Whatever you think, say, or do in that state of being—as Being itself—is an expression of divine love.

Communication is a state of *mind*, but communion is a state of *no-mind*. Communication is a state of *mind*, but communion is a state of *being*.

In fact, communion *is* Being itself.

With communication, there seem to be two separate
entities; but with communion, there is only One.

When you live from your heart instead of your head, love flows
into and out of everything you think, say, and do.

Communion is a totally different dimension.

Communication is a *thinking* thing, but communion is a *feeling* thing.

Communication is two heads meeting, but communion is two hearts
melting into One. Communion is two hearts beating so closely together
in rhythm, in unison, and in harmony that there is just One.

Communion is the felt recognition that two hearts
never existed—only One ever existed.

Namaste, my friends.

THE FORMLESS TAKING FORM

Heart-to-heart communication happens in the spirit.

In fact, it *is* the spirit.

When heart-to-heart communication is formless and wordless—when you remain silent both inside and outside—it is called "deep listening."

When heart-to-heart communication takes the form of words—when you remain silent inside, but put words to it for the outside world—it is called "loving speech."

Heart-to-heart communication is being in-tune with the peace, love, and joy inside you. It's being in tune with—feeling one with, feeling the presence of—the divine within you.

When you express that love through *silence*, it is deep, loving listening. When you express that love through *speech*, it is deep, loving speech.

Anything can become a spiritual act when it's infused with love. When anything is done with heartfelt love, it is inspired; it is "in-spirit."

It is spiritual, because it is inspired by spirit, the spirit within you, the spirit that *is* you.

•

NOTHING TO SAY, NOBODY TO SAY IT

From the highest perspective, only life is.

Only life really exists, not you and not anybody else.

When there is nobody in the room—when only life exists— there is nothing to say and nobody to say it.

There is nothing to hear and nobody to hear it.

There is nothing to know and nobody to know it.

There's just silence, and that silence sings!

There's just stillness, and that stillness dances!

There's just spaciousness, and that spaciousness celebrates!

DEEP LISTENING

Deep listening is listening from the heart.

It's listening with pure presence. It's listening *as* Presence itself.

It's listening silently, inside and out. It's listening *as* Stillness and Silence itself.

When you listen from the heart in this way, you forget yourself.
If you cannot forget yourself, you cannot really listen.

Listening from the heart—listening silently, inside and out—is listening
to the other person without filtering it through your own preconceived
ideas. It's listening to the *other* person—not listening to your own
thoughts, opinions, beliefs, and judgments about the other person.

Deep listening means not interrupting the other person, mentally or verbally. It
means not interrupting the other person with your spoken or unspoken thoughts.

To listen lovingly means not to interject your own ideas
or opinions—for or against, silently or audibly.

When you listen from the heart, you don't—can't—become
defensive. Yes, you might clarify a misunderstanding, but you will
not do so with any inner resistance, reactivity, or negativity.

Yes, you might deny something, but you will do so without becoming defensive.
You might disagree, but you will do so without being disagreeable.

In deep listening, your primary job is to be a mirror. Your principal duty is to mirror
back to the other person—objectively and impartially—what they had said to you.

You are not imposing your thoughts or feelings on the other person. You are
simply reflecting back to your friend their own ideas. Your intention is to
help them feel heard and to make sure you have heard them correctly.

In this way, you give the other person an opportunity to feel seen and
heard, hear their own wisdom, and correct any misunderstanding
or miscommunication that might have taken place.

This is called "conscious conversation," and it's the
cornerstone of all conscious relationships.

Listen without thinking about yourself... or anything else, for that matter.

Listen without thinking—that's deep listening.

LISTENING WITH AN EMPTY MIND

Love means listening.

The more you listen, the more you love; and the more you love, the more you listen.

But listening isn't something that's done with the mind—
listening is something that's done with the heart.

"Can you hear my heart?" That's love.

To love people, listen to them. Listen to them and don't be
distracted. Listen to them with nothing on your mind—without
any running commentary, without any mental chatter.

Listen to people with an empty mind—without any interpretation.
Don't think in terms of interpreting—agreeing or disagreeing,
liking or disliking—with what people have to say.

Listen without any preconception, without any expectation,
without any anticipation or impatience. Deep listening means
to listen attentively, with nothing on your mind.

To love people, listen to them the way you listen to music: playfully, easily,
and effortlessly. Listen in a relaxed, non-resistant way. Listen lovingly—
without criticizing, condemning, controlling, or trying to convince.

Listen meditatively.

The more you meditate, the more you understand how to really listen with
nothing on your mind. And the more you learn to listen with nothing on your
mind, the more heart-to-heart communication happens automatically.

Just listen without agreeing or disagreeing, without approving or
disapproving, without accepting or rejecting anything.

Just listen, that's all.

LISTENING TO KEEP LOVE ALIVE

Rumi writes, "Out beyond ideas of wrongdoing and
rightdoing there is a field. I'll meet you there."

The place Rumi is talking about is inside you.

Rumi wants to meet you in that sacred place within you where—when
you are in yours, and I am in mine—there is only One of us.

Then, of course, it's not a meeting at all—it's a melting
and merging. It's not unification, but union.

When you listen without judgment, you transcend human duality—right and
wrong, good and bad, positive and negative—and you discover divine oneness.

You transcend the human mind and discover divine no-mind.

You die to the worldly plane, and you are reborn on the spiritual plane.

Listening means staying out of your head, so you can really hear the other person's
heart. It means having a true "heart-to-heart" conversation. It means communicating
at the heart level, the level of love, not at the mind level or the level of logic.

It means listening—and living—like a Buddha, like a Jesus,
and like a Lao Tzu. It means being a person of kindness and
compassion, not a person of judgment and justice.

Listen with an open mind and an open heart.

Be willing to let what's being said change your mind and your heart. Listen
in such a way that your heart can be touched. Listen in such a way that
your heart can be moved by what the other person is saying. Listen to the
other person's heart—their light, their love—not just their words.

Listen in such a way that you keep peace, love, and joy alive inside of you.

Listen in such a way that you remain aware of the peace,
love, and joy that is always inside of you.

Listen in such a way that you remain aware of the divine inside you.

In other words, listening from the heart means listening to the other
person with a quiet mind, yes, but it also means much more than that.

Listening from the heart, ultimately, means feeling the other's presence—
which is really your own presence—while you are with them.

It means feeling Presence itself—the presence of God
within *yourself*—while you are with them.

INFORMATION OR TRANSFORMATION?

Listening to people with a quiet mind is infinitely more powerful
than anything else you can possibly think, say, or do.

More than anything you can think, say, or do, your peaceful, joyful,
loving presence—Presence itself—is what most helps.

It's not so much what you think or say that changes people—
it's *what you are* that changes people. It's not so much what you
do that heals people—it's *what you are* that heals people.

Loving people are living lights. People are drawn to them because of
the love and warmth they share through their mere presence.

Loving people are alchemists. Through their magnetic, magnanimous
presence, they alchemically transform people's entire beings!

Loving people are catalysts; they are catalytic converters.

They burn up the false you, and give birth to the original
you—the pure, clean, healthy, happy you.

Through love, you become a phoenix rising from the ashes.

Love doesn't *inform* you—it *transforms* you! Transforming,
not informing—that's what love does.

Love doesn't *educate* you—it *eradicates* you! It eradicates the ego that you think
is you. That's why Jesus says, "I did not come to bring peace, but a sword."

Spiritual teachers like Jesus and Buddha empty you of all the impurities
and toxins inside. They empty you of everything that is unhealthy
and unhappy inside, everything that is blocking love inside.

Through their mere presence alone, true spiritual teachers help you see through
the false, fearful, unfulfilled self to the real, peaceful, loving, fulfilled Self.

People might go to a Jesus or a Buddha for more information to stuff into their head,
but they leave only after having undergone a total transformation of their heart!

That's what real love does.

If you really want to help anyone, then, don't only try to give them more
information, more advice, or more guidance—instead, think bigger!

Work to transform them through your peaceful, joyful, loving presence. Transform them through your light and love, not your logic.

True transformation happens in, of, and through the heart—the spiritual heart, not the head.

It happens through Presence, not personhood. It happens through the Presence within a person, not through a person him or herself.

It happens through Presence, not personality. It happens though God (within), not the ego.

It happens through no-mind, not mind.

It happens through meditation, not argumentation.

BE THE CHANGE

Stop giving people unsolicited advice, particularly your partner.

Teach them through your living, shining example, instead.

You can *show* them better than you can tell them.

Drop this whole idea that you know something that other people don't know, and just decide to *be* something that other people aren't being.

If you really want to help people, your partner included, leave your logic at the doorstep and love people, instead.

There's nothing more helpful to the world than your peaceful, loving, joyful presence. What the world needs more than anything else is more peaceful, loving, joyful people.

Studies show that the most effective element of therapy is unconditional regard. It's been found that unconditional regard is transformative all by itself; it changes people all by itself.

If you want to help people, teach them, through the clarity of your living, shining example. Teach them through the power of your peaceful, loving, joyful presence how to *be* peace, *be* love, and *be* joy, too!

SPEAK LESS TO SAY MORE

Meditation is the art of becoming more and more silent inside.

Keep silent sometimes.

Then, when you speak, your words will have real value.

Speech is most valuable once you have attained silence. When you've attained silence, your words will pack a much more powerful punch.

In other words, before you speak, meditate.

Quiet your mind completely. Then, you will understand—and be able to speak to—the nature of things at a much deeper level.

If you do that, you will be much more likely to say only what is true, helpful, inspiring, necessary, and kind.

When in doubt, however, this little acronym can be helpful to remember: **THINK**.

Before you speak, remember to **THINK**.

That means to only say what is:

True;

Helpful;

Inspiring;

Necessary; and

Kind.

In other words, ask yourself: "How can I say what I want to say in a way that is just as true as what I originally planned to say...but is also more helpful, more inspiring, and kinder than what I was originally planning to say?

Often, the more you say, the less you communicate. Too many words sometimes dilute the power of your words. Fewer words often pack a bigger, more powerful punch.

Speak less to say more.

USING YOUR PRESENCE

Not long ago, I was at the grocery store doing some shopping.

While there, I overheard a conversation between a mother and her daughter. The little girl was five or six years old, and she was having a temper tantrum. She was crying about something.

She was begging her mom for something, but her mom just wouldn't give in to the little girl's demands. The little girl's frustration was infectious; it was spreading to the mom.

But, then, in a moment of absolute clarity, coolness, and composure, the little girl's mom said something that worked wonders on the situation.

She said, "Savannah, use your words, honey. Just use your words."

I thought that was brilliant. Yes, when you're upset, don't just have a screaming fit. Don't just have a temper tantrum. Use your words.

I liked what that mother said that day, and I've come up with something that I like even better.

When you really want to say something in a powerful way, don't just use your words—use your *presence*. Don't just use your words—use your *silence*.

"Using your presence" or "using your silence" means resting your mind, so that it will be sharper and more powerful when you are ready to use it.

REST THE MIND, REST IN THE DIVINE

By "rest the mind," I mean "watch the mind."

I mean be the watcher or observer of the mind. I mean be
the thoughtless awareness behind the mind.

Don't try to stop a thought—that's not what I mean. The very effort
to stop a thought feeds it. It gives it energy. The very effort to
avoid a thought or feeling only fuels it and keeps it going.

Don't try to stop the mind—there is no need to stop the mind. Just watch
the mind. Just observe your thoughts and feelings without judgment.

Everything comes and goes. Just remain a watch⸱ ⸱⸱n the hill.
Don't identify with anything—good, bad, or indiffere⸱ ⸱

That's what I mean by "rest the mind."

By "rest the mind," I mean rest in thoughtless awareness.

By "rest the mind," I mean rest in peace, love, and joy.

I mean rest in Presence, the presence of God (within).

Once your mind knows how to rest, it becomes powerful. Then its words aren't just
words—they are arrows! They are arrows that penetrate the heart of the other. Your
words suddenly have a richness, clarity, and quality that they never had before.

Rest the mind so that when you speak, you'll only say that which is helpful. Rest
the mind so that you'll only share what you've experienced. Of course, what you
will have experienced more than anything else will be peace, love, and joy.

When you rest your mind, it is a divine rest. And in that divine
rest, your thoughts, words, and ways become divine ones!

When you become still and silent inside, you become a hollow bamboo shoot
for the divine. You become life's flute. A divine melody courses through
your veins, and nothing but divine music parts from your mouth.

Using your emotions is animalistic; using your words
is human; but using your presence is divine!

Rest your mind, rest in the divine!

WAIT AND MEDITATE,
MEDITATE AND MOVE!

Here's something to remember...

Try not to have important conversations or make important decisions
when you are feeling less than peaceful, joyful, or loving.

Instead, wait—wait and meditate!

Wait until you feel better to have those crucial
conversations and make those difficult decisions.

When you wait and meditate, your mood rises all by itself.

Before long and with minimal effort, you'll find yourself in a better position
to have those crucial conversations and make those difficult decisions.

Then, your conversations and decisions will lead to smarter, more
creative, more productive, and altogether happier outcomes.

Before every important conversation, decision, and action, let there be a moment
of meditation. Before you do whatever you do, close your eyes, be silent, and
go within. Look as an observer—unattached, unprejudiced, and impartial.

Then, when the timing feels right, move!

Lao Tzu says, "Do you have the patience to wait till your mind settles and the
water is clear? Can you remain unmoving till the right action arises by itself?"

When you meditate, you can hear your heart, your spiritual heart.
You can hear your intuition, your inner guidance system. You can
hear that still, small voice within. You can hear 'God' within.

Then, the right words, decisions, and actions arise on their own.

That's what I mean when I say, "Wait and meditate" or "Meditate and, then, move."

Jesus says it this way, "Seek first the kingdom of God
and the rest will be added unto you."

In other words, focus on feeling the presence of the divine—the peace, love, and joy—within you. Spend time communing with the divine for its own sake, for joy's sake, for love's sake alone.

Then, everything else will take care of itself. Everything else will show up. It will all be added.

Chapter 12

FINAL NON-THOUGHTS

DON'T TALK ABOUT IT, BE ABOUT IT!

Do you spend a lot of time thinking and talking
about your love life... or lack thereof?

Do you think you can figure him or her—your partner or potential partner—out?

Do you think you can solve your relationship problems—and fix your
love life—by thinking and talking about it all over and over again?

Here's the thing: Like life itself, love is not a problem to be solved—
it's an adventure to be lived and a mystery to be enjoyed!

Love can't be understood intellectually. You have to do more
than just think or talk about love to understand it.

You have to *experience* it for yourself. Love is an experience—
experience is the only explanation.

You have to *live* it to understand it—love is *lived*, or it's not love at all.

The word "water" won't make you wet, and the word "love" won't get you loved.

In other words, to know love, you have to *taste* it. You have to drink it.
You have to imbibe it. You have to get drunk off of it yourself!

Real love can't be talked about. If it could be talked about, it wouldn't be real
love. Real love is ineffable—it can't be reduced to thoughts or words.

You can't talk about it, but you can dance it! You
can't think about it, but you can sing it!

Love is not something you can think or talk about—
love is something you have to *be* about!

It's true: "Saying [or thinking] a thing a thousand
times is not as good as living it once."

Love doesn't live in your head—love lives in your heart. It's
poetry, not prose. It's music, not mathematics.

In other words, love is not what you think. In fact, it's not what *anybody* thinks.

Love is what happens when you *don't* think.

Love is an experience in your heart—not an explanation in your head.

LOVE IS MORE THAN A NOTION

My mom has an expression that she uses sometimes.

She says, "I'll tell you, that is more than a notion!"

When my mom uses that expression, she is almost always referring
to somebody who is being naïve about something.

Maybe it's a young girl who wants a baby before she's ready. Maybe it's
a young man who wants to buy a house or car that he can't afford.

She can be referring to a thousand and one things, but, ultimately, she always
means the same thing: There's a lot more to that—whatever "that" is—than
you think. There's a lot more involved than you've been led to believe.

"It's more than a notion!"

And that's the essential message here, too: There's more to love
than what you think; love is more than what you think it is.

People have all kinds of ideas about what it means to love, but most of those ideas
are just that: ideas. They are ideas without any basis in reality or real-life experience.

I've lived long enough to know one thing: Love, real love, is not
something you think about—it's something you live.

To *experience* love, you have to let go of your ideas, especially
your ideas about love. You have to drop what you think you
know about love so that you can experience love for real.

To know, you have to let go of what you *think* you know. To find
divine wisdom, you have to give up human knowledge.

In other words, divine wisdom always seems foolish to the human mind.

Lao Tzu agrees. He says, "True wisdom seems foolish."

The Bible agrees, too. It says, "'For the wisdom of this world is foolishness to God.'
As the Scriptures say, 'He traps the wise in the snare of their own cleverness.'
And again, 'God knows the thoughts of the wise; he knows they are worthless.'"

Never forget it: Love only happens when you are able to let
go of everything you think you know about love.

In other words, love grows out of meditation, and meditation is not learning—it's *unlearning*. It's unlearning everything you've been taught about love.

Lao Tzu says it this way: "To attain knowledge, add things every day. To attain wisdom, remove things every day."

Love is not learning—it's *unlearning*.

Love is not logical—it's *illogical*.

Love is not a state of mind—it's a state of *being*.

In fact, it's Being itself.

NOTHING GOOD OR BAD

Shakespeare is famous for saying, "There is nothing
either good or bad, but thinking makes it so."

Nothing has any inherent meaning—good or bad, right or wrong,
positive or negative—in and of itself. It's only our mind that assigns
value and attaches meaning to things. It's only our mind that judges
right and wrong, good and evil, positive and negative.

It's only our mind that lives—*believes* it lives—in duality.
It's only our mind that creates duality.

In Reality, there is nothing but non-duality; there is nothing but oneness.

What is "original sin" but this belief in duality? What is original sin but the belief in
separation? What is original sin but eating from the tree of knowledge of good and
evil and, as a result of that, seeing separation where before only oneness existed?

In other words, what is it except thinking that ever separates us from—gives
us the *illusion* that we could ever be separated from—life and all life forms,
from God and each other? What is it but thinking that ever misleads us
into believing that we could ever be separate from anything or anybody?

Love, then, means going beyond your belief in duality; it
means going beyond your belief in separation.

Love means dropping your ideas of separation—your judgments of
good and evil, right and wrong, positive and negative—so that you can
enter into the experience of oneness, of love, right here and now.

THINK LESS, LOVE MORE

Think less—*live* more!

Think less—*love* more!

Don't try to understand life so much—just live it.

Don't try to understand love so much—just move into it.

Then, you will know it by experiencing it.

In other words, meditate the way Maharaji, the Indian mystic,
said Jesus meditated: "He drowned himself in love!"

Think less and meditate more.

Think less and drown yourself in love. Think less and drown yourself in life
(God) and felt oneness with life (love)—that's what "to meditate" really means.

With love, the key is to spend less time thinking and talking about it—
what it is, what it isn't, and what it should be—and more time *being* it.

You can't appreciate what you're too busy analyzing, and
you can't enjoy what you're too busy examining.

Analyze less—appreciate more. Evaluate less—enjoy more.

Think less—live more! Think less—laugh more! Think less—love more!

"MELTS IN YOUR MOUTH,
NOT IN YOUR HAND"

Do you remember those old M&M candy commercials:
"It melts in your mouth, not in your hand"?

Yes, that is exactly right. Love is exactly like that.

M&Ms melt in your mouth, not in your hand, and love,
too, melts in your mouth, not in your hand.

When you talk about love, love is no longer love—it is just
hot air. When you talk about love, it melts in your mouth—it
disappears. It evaporates. You destroy your experience of it.

When you only think and talk about love—and don't *live* it—love ceases to
exist as love. But when you live *as* love—when you live a life of love, when
you exist in a state of love—love remains. Love lives on in your experience.

Love melts in your mouth, not in your hand!

When you just talk about love, love melts in your mouth; but when you are a
loving person—when love is your state of being, when you extend a helping hand
out of love, for instance—love remains. Your experience of love continues.

Love melts in your mouth, not in your hand!

Don't talk about it—*be* about it! Don't think about it—*be* about it!

Don't let love be only in your mouth—let it be in your heart and
hand, too. Let it be in the way you live your life, too.

But that's not the whole metaphor...

M&Ms melt in your mouth, not in your hand, but that's only if you keep an
open hand. If you close your hand, the M&Ms *will* melt in your hand, too.

Likewise, love melts in your mouth, not in your hand,
but that's only if you keep an open hand!

Love is an open-hand—no grasping, no clinging, no attachment, no judgment,
no expectations, no guarantees. Love is freedom, complete freedom.

Love melts in your mouth, not in your *open* hand.

Don't hold on—let go.

Don't close down—open up.

Don't tighten up—loosen up and relax!

ONE LOVE

When you love somebody, you merge with them.

Something between you becomes a bridge.

In fact, you realize that you have always been one with them.

So, there is no need for any bridge.

One life, one heart, one soul.

One love.

•

MAKING ROOM FOR LOVE

Jesus says, "Blessed are the poor in spirit, for theirs is the kingdom of heaven."

Love only happens to those who are empty of—or, at least, unimpressed with—their own thoughts. When you are full of your own thoughts, there is no room for love.

When you're full of too many thoughts, true love is impossible for you. No matter how hard you try and no matter what you think, you will never experience true love with a mind full of thoughts.

But when you are empty of your own thoughts, you become an empty room—a spacious, sacred temple—for love to enter.

In fact, you realize that you've always been an empty room—a spacious, sacred temple—where love lives.

CONCLUSION

DIVINE DISCONTENTMENT

Sometimes, hope can be a hurdle to happiness. In certain cases, hope can be an obstacle to love.

And if you focus only on the hope of meeting a lover one day, you focus exclusively on the future. If you focus exclusively on the future, you miss this precious, prosperous present moment. You miss the love and happiness that is available to you here and now.

Hope—hoping for a lover, hoping for better health, hoping for somebody to change, hoping for more money, hoping for a better tomorrow, hoping for anything—can't makes us happy now, and it can't make us feel loved now, either.

Hope is great, but hope can never make us feel truly happy. Hope is great, but if you're not careful, hope can get in the way of being happy and feeling loved right here and now.

The point isn't to deny hope, but to declare that hope alone isn't enough. Every moment can and should be a moment of love and happiness all on its own. Love and happiness shouldn't just be saved for future moments. Love and happiness should be experienced and enjoyed today.

In other words, please be careful of living only for your future dreams. Too many people's dreams keep them focused on the future, but life can only be lived, loved, and enjoyed in the present. A dream is something that can and should be lived *today*, right here and now—not later.

Life knows nothing of the future; life has never heard of it. We all create the future in our minds, and we go on living in this illusory, mind-made future, sacrificing the present. We miss the gift that is life, love, and happiness.

Divine despair is needed! Are you totally dissatisfied with the world and its inability to give you what you really want: love and happiness? You have to be completely dissatisfied with the world before you can go in search of—and find—something deeper and more divine, something altogether more fulfilling within.

Are you really dissatisfied? You might be dissatisfied with this or that, with this person or that person, but are you totally dissatisfied with the world, as such? Are you still looking for satisfaction—love and happiness—somewhere else other than this time and place, in somebody other than yourself?

Divine discontent is necessary! Are you totally hopeless? You might feel hopeless because certain things haven't happened in your life, but you still hope. You have to become fed up with hope itself, so that you can go in search of something altogether more promising, meaningful, and fulfilling.

Until you understand this simple thing—that love and happiness are found right here and now inside you or not at all—nothing and nobody can help you. A guru can give you a thousand and one methods, but they will not help you. A lover can shower you with countless gifts, but they will not save you.

If you don't understand this basic thing—that you are not in the world but the world is *in you*—those methods will just be escape mechanisms, and those gifts will just be distraction techniques. And no real joy can be found in escaping or distraction.

You can go to the moon, but all of your problems will just follow you. You'll be sitting on the moon wondering why your lover doesn't love you more. You'll be sitting on Mars wondering why you're still not married... or happy. All of those methods and gifts will just help you avoid the one thing you need to change your life: yourself.

Of course, the irony is that, once you understand this, not a single additional thing is needed, not a single method is necessary. Everything just starts happening on its own accord.

Just an understanding and miracles happen—you will be surprised. Just by understanding something deep in your heart, your life will be transformed forever. And, then, all kinds of wonderful, miraculous things—like the right people showing up—will start happening to you.

Like Buddha and like Jesus, flowers will start showering down on you from heaven. It's the greatest secret nobody has ever told you: *Everything you've been looking for is right here inside of you!*

LOVE NOW!

When you are deeply aware that you could die any moment—that this breath could be your last—you don't put your love life on hold any longer. You find somebody or something—anybody or anything—to love right here and now. You find some reason—any reason—to be happy this red-hot moment. You don't wait, and you don't procrastinate!

People talk about wanting to live happily-ever-after—and be in love forever—but that's stupid, because you can't control the future, and you can't control other people.

Looking for love outside of yourself, instead of within yourself... and in the future, instead of the present... is the cause of all the suffering in the world. Love isn't found in the world—it is found within you. It isn't found in the future—it is found in the present.

If you are always running after something or somebody "out there," you are looking for love where it doesn't exist. That is a sure way to never find it.

To find love, you have to learn to live in the present, in Presence itself. If you can't live in the present, in Presence itself, you can't relax. And if you can't relax, you can't find love, because tension blocks love.

So, always remember: love isn't found in any person, place, or thing or in the future. It is found within yourself, here and now. It is found in Presence—"now-here"—or "nowhere" at all!

HAPPILY-EVER-AFTER BEGINS TODAY

Do you want to live happily ever after? Do you want to "be in love forever?" Are you still hoping to find love in the future?

You don't even have access to the next moment—what can be said about tomorrow, next week, or next year? You don't have access to the future—how can you possibly control it? By the time the future gets to you, it is already the present.

No, you can't even put a single finger on the future. All you can control is the present, and even that is debatable. The most you can do is control yourself in the present, and even that is questionable.

Happily-ever-after? Forever? Come on!

People aren't even happy right now, and they're thinking about being happy tomorrow! People aren't even loving themselves right now, and they're worried about other people—people whom they haven't even met yet—loving them tomorrow! People don't even love who is in their life right now, including themselves, and they're thinking about loving—or being loved by—somebody for a lifetime!

Forget about the future—focus on now!

If you take care of today, tomorrow will take care of itself, because tomorrow will grow out of today. If today is full of peace, love, and happiness, tomorrow will be, too. If today is a blessing and a benediction, tomorrow will be an even greater blessing and benediction. If today is blissful, tomorrow will be even more blissful.

Let me repeat this, because it's so important: Wanting to "live happily-ever-after" and be loved by one person forever, in the way most people mean it, is silly. For one, the future is uncontrollable. For two, people are uncontrollable. Haven't you noticed?

You can't even control yourself for a few moments, say during meditation, so what makes you think you can control others? You don't even love *yourself* right now, so what makes you think you can make somebody else love you forever? Even if you could make somebody love you forever, is that the kind of love you want—forced? Is forced love real love? Is forced love even love at all?

No, if you put your peace, love, and happiness in the hands of other people, you will always be disappointed. If you put your love life in the hands of other people, you will always be frustrated.

Your love life depends on you and you only. It's not anybody else's job to love you—that's your job! It's not anybody else's responsibility to make you happy—that's your responsibility!

ACKNOWLEDGEMENTS

I'D LIKE TO THANK THE PHENOMENAL TEAM AT MANGO Publishing, including Brenda Knight, who spearheaded the overall publishing effort; Yaddyra Peralta, who managed the editing process; Robin Miller, who polished the final product; Katia Mena, who created the beautiful layout; and the rest of the Mango team, who worked tirelessly behind the scenes to bring this book to fruition.

ABOUT THE AUTHOR

ROBERT MACK IS AN IVY-LEAGUE-EDUCATED, DEPTH POSITIVE psychology expert, celebrity happiness coach, executive coach, and author.

Robert studied under the direction of Martin Seligman, the founder of Positive Psychology, at the University of Pennsylvania (UPenn). UPenn is the only institution in the world to offer a Masters degree in Applied Positive Psychology.

After suffering from depression and suicidal ideation for over twenty years, Robert experienced a profound awakening. Soon thereafter, he devoted his life to deepening, integrating, and sharing that transformative experience with others who were also seeking an end to their suffering.

Robert's work has been endorsed by Oprah, Vanessa Williams, and many others, and he has been seen on *Good Morning America*, *The Today Show*, *Access Hollywood*, E!, OWN, GQ, *Self*, *Health*, *Cosmopolitan*, and *Glamour*.

Robert's first book, *Happiness from the Inside Out: The Art and Science of Fulfillment*, is celebrity-endorsed and critically acclaimed. It has been translated into various languages, including Chinese.

Robert coaches individuals from all walks of life—including professional athletes, popular entertainers, senior executives, and everyday people—and he consults with organizations of all types and sizes, such as Google, YouTube, Facebook, Twilio, Microsoft, SalesForce, Deloitte Consulting, Capital One, and many others.

Prior to his current work, Robert worked as a Big 5 management consultant and, then, as a professional model and actor. He's worked for clients like Nike, Reebok, Nordstrom, Neiman Marcus, Sandals Resorts, St. Kitts Tourism, and Toys-R-Us. He also played "Paco" on the CW's short-lived TV series, *South Beach*.

You can learn more about Robert and his work by exploring his website (www.coachrobmack.com) or by connecting with him on social media (@robmackofficial).

Mango Publishing, established in 2014, publishes an eclectic list of books by diverse authors—both new and established voices—on topics ranging from business, personal growth, women's empowerment, LGBTQ studies, health, and spirituality to history, popular culture, time management, decluttering, lifestyle, mental wellness, aging, and sustainable living. We were recently named 2019 and 2020's #1 fastest-growing independent publisher by Publishers Weekly. Our success is driven by our main goal, which is to publish high-quality books that will entertain readers as well as make a positive difference in their lives.

Our readers are our most important resource; we value your input, suggestions, and ideas. We'd love to hear from you—after all, we are publishing books for you!

Please stay in touch with us and follow us at:
Facebook: Mango Publishing
Twitter: @MangoPublishing
Instagram: @MangoPublishing
LinkedIn: Mango Publishing
Pinterest: Mango Publishing
Newsletter: mangopublishinggroup.com/newsletter

Join us on Mango's journey to reinvent publishing, one book at a time.

CPSIA information can be obtained
at www.ICGtesting.com
Printed in the USA
JSHW051725280322
24354JS00002B/2